Manufacturing Standard Costing Practical Handbook

A pragmatic handbook with complete solutions

CONSTANCE HOLTZHAUSEN FCCA MBA
BSC. (HONS)

DEDICATION

I would like to dedicate this book to my mum.

I am so pleased and proud to call such a distinguished and super-woman my mum.

No matter how difficult financially things were at times, my mum was always kind and generous to everyone she came in contact with, especially those who had less.

My mum was inspirational, which I only came to notice as an adult. As a child saw my mum working so hard to look after the family. She used to have a "provision store" what is now called a convenience store, where she sold beverages, including sweets and doughnuts and she used to get up at 4 am every morning to bake the doughnuts. She was the first person to show me that "work is fun".

FOREWARD

I would like to thank Michael Smith as my mentor. Also, for his advice throughout the project and comments on earlier drafts, including proofreading the English version of this document, as there is also a German-language version.

Table of Contents

INTRODUCTION

A re you not surprised sometimes to read about your favourite company filing for insolvency when they should be in black?

Let me ask you these following questions:

- Does your team know how to use standard costs for product costing, inventory valuation and control?
- Can your team set and review standard cost Bills of material and routings?
- Analyse and verify your monthly labour utilization and efficiency variances, and able to review and investigate purchase price and material usage variances?
- Can you develop and monitor labour and overhead rates for departments/cost centre?
- Does your controller know how to investigate and analysing sales and cost of sales, labour reporting, product costing, and material usage variances?
- Do you know the right reports to use when analysing standard manufacturing variances against actuals?

If your answer is no, then this book is what you need, as it would provide you with the necessary assistance in setting standard costs for your products and services costing and the valuation of your inventories.

THE INTENDED AUDIENCE

The book is intended primarily for cost accountants, controllers, engineers, buyers, management to be used as a guide to making policies and procedures for setting standard costs, which subsequently would influence significantly the decisions, actions, and activities taken by the management for the day-to-day running of the operations. It's also intended as a handbook for those whose job is to plan and analyse.

SCOPE OF BOOK

The scope of this book is by itself the title, "Manufacturing Standard Costing Handbook". It's the use of standard costs for product costing. It's used to identify, implement various corrective measures, which would help businesses to improve the costs of goods sold of their products, margin and for the strategic decision-making of your management team.

For the sake of simplicity, and conciseness, the topic in this book would go as far as the essential elements of standard costs as follows:

- Raw materials and packaging components cost
- Direct labour and benefits
- Manufacturing/processing and filling/assembly cost centre charge
- Human resources burden
- Stock-keeping unit (SKU)/Volume-related burden
- Materials warehouse burden
- Purchased finished goods/contract labour

- Internally-produced packaging
- Non-production loss provision

In a nutshell, would specify the essential elements of the manufacturing costs as shown below:

- Direct material: contains all material component that forms an integral part of the finished product or which contributes to the fabrication and conversion of such materials.
- Direct labour: can directly assigned to a particular item produced or which contributes directly to the fabrication of such product.
- Factory Overhead: contains all other manufacturing cost that cannot directly identified to a given product such as indirect labour, factory supplies.

However, I shall not be concentrating in great details on analysing variances. Instead, I shall be focusing accurately in identifying the various kinds of expenses, the formula for the various cost standards and how to calculate the costs.

HOW THIS BOOK CAME ABOUT

Having qualified as a Fellow Chartered Certified Accountant, including obtaining an MBA degree in the UK, together with my international exposure working for manufacturing, automotive and other industry, I found myself training and coaching the finance departments and German Controllers. I have the privilege to work as a consultant mainly for German subsidiaries of United States or

United Kingdom parent companies, where some of my responsibilities have included the following:

- Responsible for the coordination, administration and analysis of manufacturing operations (analysing sales and cost of sales, labour reporting, product costing, and monthly material usage variances and inventory adjustments)
- Developed and monitored labour and overhead rates for department/cost centre
- Worked with industrial engineering to insure cost and rate accuracy
- Reviewed the cost routings for reasonableness
- Responsible for the analysis of product costs, overhead absorption, abnormal fixed cost expenditures, etc

I was also responsible for comparing actual to standard manufacturing variance analysis as follows:

- Analyse and verified the monthly labour utilisation and efficiency

- Reviewed and investigated purchase price and material usage variances

In some of my various assignments, I've noticed that one of the common issues is the lack of setting the correct standard costs for product costing, which in return give rise to variances.

I want to use this book together with my experience to help you, companies, controllers, cost accountants, engineers, etc., use in the compilation of various cost elements used in the calculation of standard cost for your product costing. This book provides a step-by-step guide for calculating standard cost of raw material/packaging, equipment costs, production volumes, and efficient methods of production.

Standard costs can only be as accurate as the budget or latest sales forecast volume, projected production expenses, and forecast raw material price increases, only if the use of the correct standard cost is in place. At the same time, it's essential that sales, marketing, production, purchasing, and finance teams, see this preparation of standard costs as a joint effort with shared responsibility for accuracy.

MAJOR SOURCES

The topics in the book and material appearing in the appendices are, based on the author's recollections of her studies with the association of chartered certified accountants (ACCA), and her experience and observation while working as a senior finance professional.

HOW TO USE THIS BOOK

This book is divided into three main sections, with each section containing couple of chapters. The table below explains the key element of each sections.

Text	Sections	Importance
Introduction	This section summaries the audience that the book is intended to benefit from the book. It also covers the extent and scope the book covers.	It describes the objectives of this book and the importance of using standard costs to cost your product or services, and most importantly, how practical experience helped to write this book.
Chapter 1-2	General and costing Procedure which could be used in setting the standards.	Where adequate general or standard costing procedure does not exist, the company should not attempt to use a procedure that is not the same as the one in this book, because using a procedure which was not designed for the purpose of accurately costing your products just like the examples in this book may have unforeseeable and undesirable results.

Chapter 3	It highlights the kind of direct materials and their expenses which are used to create finished goods formula.	Failure to calculate the correct raw material would cause an inaccurate cost estimate and profit forecasts would not be accurate.
Chapter 4	It highlights the type of activities that should be classed, under direct labour and benefits, including the calculation.	The misclassification of these costs could harm your overall costs per unit and would be a challenge to compete against your competitors.
Chapter 5	The expenses that are associated with the area used by the manufacturing processes, such as, pressing processing/assembly or inspection cost centre charges.	As failure to calculate the number of units and machine hours required/ costs per machine hours would have an adverse effect on the total production costs.
Chapter 6	The HR burden is the allocation of general services and HR expenses supporting the manufacturing operation.	Failure to track and calculate these overheads would lead to under-absorption of costs, and that is if you're using absorption costing for your valuation.

Chapter 7	The SKU/Volume Related Burden are the expenses of plant operations management.	Again, part of the factory overhead. The total of this burden and it's divided by the estimated number of production run.
Chapter 8	These are the expenses related to receiving and storing of raw and packaging materials, including warehouse personnel.	Just like any other factory overhead, where the total costs should be divided by estimated physical units/cases to determine cost/unit. Failure would result to under-absorption of overheads.
Text	**Sections**	**Importance**
Chapter 9	This type of cost relates to production processes and indirect labour that are outsourced by 3rd-party vendors.	This type of cost, including fees charged by the vendors, should be included in the standard cost of a product, as otherwise, it might cause adverse variance between actual and standard.
Chapter 10	The prime and conversion (direct material, direct labour	This chapter summarises Chapters 2 – 9. It includes

| | costs, including variable and fixed overhead. | some examples using the absorption and marginal cost. Absorption cost absorbs both direct material and factory overhead into the product cost, while marginal cost uses only the direct or variable costs. |
| Chapter 11 | Variance Analysis | This chapter focuses on variance analysis. There are two types of cost Variances: spending (price) variances and quantity (usage or efficiency) variances. The spending variances includes (direct materials, direct labour, and variable overhead), while usage variances calculate the variable manufacturing costs, and followed by the spending and usage variances for fixed overhead. |

| Chapter 12 | Record Retention | It focuses on retaining your documents. |
| Chapter 13 | Conclusion | Summaries the importance of maintain standard cost system. |

CHAPTER 1

GENERAL PROCEDURE

In general, the product cost standard represents in long-run cost of production for an item for the specified periods. If current conditions prevent the attainment of a business long-run cost for an item or items (e.g. significant overcapacity), then you might want to review your historical product costs as it could have included the cost of unused capacity already (i.e. excess depreciation, occupancy, and other costs).

At a minimum, all standard costs should be updated either semi-annually (from July – December and January – June periods) or annually. More frequent revisions are at the discretion of local management, taking into consideration the cost/benefit of making such changes.

The use of local currency cost standards for product costing and inventory valuation is recommended for all subsidiaries except for hyperinflation countries. Hyperinflationary countries not using constant currency should consider establishing standards in a stable currency, such as Euros, GBP or U.S. Dollar.

Asset life and depreciation periods for management purposes should be standardised per IFRS, US GAAP and HGB standard. Besides, historical asset values and depreciation should be used (exception, countries reporting in constant currency should continue to revalue depreciation). This will eliminate costing differences that exist solely due to the management of depreciation.

Exhibit 1: Asset Life and Depreciation Method.

For example, let's say you purchase a piece of equipment for €250.000, and you anticipate using the equipment for 10 years, and you anticipate the scrap value would be €50.000. The calculation for depreciation of the vehicle under the straight-line method would be:

€250.000 – €50.000) / 10 = €20.000

€20,000 / 12 months = €1,666,67/month

Each month of the year, you would make the following journal entry in your accounting system:

Debit	Depreciation expense	€1,666,67
Credit	Accumulated Depreciation: Equipment (Note: In German GAAP, the accumulated depreciation account doesn't exist; instead, it's deducted in the balance sheet original value).	€1,666,67

ELEMENTS OF STANDARD COSTS

CHAPTER 2

STANDARD COSTS PROCEDURE

All manufacturing company would have first and foremost the following cost divisions:

a) Direct material

The direct material are those materials used directly in the manufacturing of products, i.e. materials that can be identified in the final products. Example, in the manufacture of chairs, the direct materials would consist of timber, nails, glue etc.

b) Direct labour

The direct labour are wages paid to those who are directly involved in the manufacturing of a product, for example, in the manufacturing of chairs, the direct labour costs would consist of wages paid to those workers who would saw, shape or join the pieces of timber into a chair.

c) Direct expenses

These are expenses that have to be incurred in the manufacturing of a product. That is, they can be directly allocated to a particular unit of a product, for example, charges for a particular equipment used in the process of manufacture, royalties.

NB: The sum of all the direct costs is known as prime costs.

d) Indirect manufacturing costs/factory overheads

These are any other expenses (apart from the direct costs) for manufactured items, for example, cleaners' wages, factory rents, depreciation of plant and equipment, factory power and lighting.

NB: prime cost + indirect manufacturing costs = PRODUCTION COSTS.

Now that we have established what production costs are, the standards are set mainly from the essential elements shown below:

A. Raw materials and packaging components cost

B. Direct labour and benefits

C. Manufacturing/processing and filling/assembly cost centre charge

D. Human resources burden (A manufacturing overhead rate used to allocate, apply and assign indirect product costs to items manufactured)

E. Stock-keeping unit (SKU)/Volume-related burden

F. Materials warehouse burden

G. Purchased finished goods/contract manufacturer

Exhibit 2.1: Cost Classification

Costs Classification		Overhead		
Description	Direct	Indirect	Burden	Overhead
Raw Material & Packaging	✓	X	X	X
Indirect Material	X	✓	X	X
Production Direct Labour & Benefits	✓	X	X	X
Manufacturing/Processing Direct Labour	✓	X	X	X
Filling/Assembly Direct Labour	✓	X	X	X
Manufacturing/Processing Cost Centre Charges	X	X	X	✓
Filling/Assembly Cost Centre Charges	X	X	X	✓
Human Resources Burden	X	X	✓	X
SKU/Volume-Related Burden	X	X	✓	X
Material Warehouse Burden	X	X	✓	X
Purchased Finished	✓	X	X	X
Contract Manufacturer + FG/WIP + Assembly	✓	X	X	X
Internal Cost of managing Contract Manufacturer Relationship	X	X	X	✓

CHAPTER 3

RAW MATERIALS AND PACKAGING COMPONENTS COSTS

DEFINITION:

The delivered cost of all materials purchased (including any inbound freight) to create the finished goods formula, ship, and dispense the product. This includes bulk purchase discount, any portion of any up-front expenses required to assure material supplies or qualify materials, such as fees, printing set-up charges, label plate charges, moulding/tooling, etc. (up-front capital required to assure material supplies or qualify materials should be capitalised and expensed over the life of the purchase agreement or project life).

Generally speaking, royalties paid for access to materials or components should be included in the materials price. They'll include, all anticipated rebates or price reductions regardless of the cause that are reasonably estimable should be included in the standard cost of materials and packaging. This definition doesn't include general production materials unless they are specifically included in the formula below, such as;

- Solid auxiliary materials (e.g. tape, staples, screws, nails, welding rods, rubber, plastics or materials of any kind, etc.).

- Liquid additives (e.g. glue, preservatives, adhesives, dyes or the large group of additives).

- Packaging material which are essential for the saleability of a product, and which is included in the selling price (e.g. food, beverages) is also an auxiliary material).

3.1 MATERIAL COST STANDARD

The material standard cost is an estimated inflated weighted average delivered cost for the period the standard is in effect. For example, if a material's weighted cost is EUR 1,00 per kilo on July 1, and is projected by purchasing and finance to cost EUR 1,10 per kilo after a price increase on October 1, the standard cost to be used for the July-December period (if the item is to be purchased regularly) is EUR 1,075. If multiple suppliers are used, for instance, the standard should be a weighted average of the suppliers' prices.

3.2 FINISHED GOODS STANDARD:

The standard cost of raw materials and packaging components in finished goods should be determined using the product formula requirement in your bill of materials and your standard cost card.

3.3 INDIRECT MATERIALS:

These are generally those materials used to further the manufacturing process, and which cannot be traced into the end product, such as glue, oil, tape, etc. They also include some materials that are contained in small quantities which are in the end product as part of indirect costs.

The following is a summary of a standard cost card or bills of material. An actual card would contain individual detail components in the product (i.e. BOM & Routing):

Exhibit 3.1: Bills of Material Card

Part No.	Need	QTY	Material Needed	Cost Level	Direct Mat.Cost	Direct Lab. Cost	Indirect Lab. Cost	Manufact. O/Heads	Direct Mach.Hr.	Fixed Expense
			STANDARD COST FORM (BILL OF MATERIALS)							
				1						
XYZ1	0		ASSEMBLY OF COMPLETE TABLE	64 €	0 €	39 €	19 €	7 €	0 €	0 €
XYZ2	1		A/ROULETTE TABLE TOP COMPLETE ASSEMBLY	0 €	0 €	0 €	0 €	0 €	0 €	0 €
XYZ3	2	1 set	WHEEL SURROUND BRASS, A/R TABLE L/H.	136 €	136 €	0 €	0 €	0 €	0 €	0 €
XYZ3	3		LEGS	0 €	0 €	0 €	0 €	0 €	0 €	0 €
XYZ3	4		FOOT RAIL	0 €	0 €	0 €	0 €	0 €	0 €	0 €
WXYZ4	5	1 set	DRINK HOLDER & ASHTRAY SOLID BRASS	154 €	154 €	0 €	0 €	0 €	0 €	0 €
WXYZ4	6		AIR RAILS	0 €	0 €	0 €	0 €	0 €	0 €	0 €
WXYZ4	7		CHIP RAILS	0 €	0 €	0 €	0 €	0 €	0 €	0 €
	8		PACKING	0 €	0 €	0 €	0 €	0 €	0 €	0 €
			This Level Cost	354 €	290 €	39 €	19 €	7 €	0 €	0 €

3.4 LOSS PROVISION FACTOR:

A loss provision factor should also be included in the calculation to account for all the raw material and packaging material losses in the production process, such as production scrap, waste, spoilage, defectives, overfill, inherent losses, etc. If these losses are significant, a separate provision for non-production losses should be established.

3.5 TREATMENT OF MATERIAL LOSSES:

3.5.1 LOSSES THROUGH WASTE:

Waste is inherent in any manufacturing activity. Waste is a part of raw material lost in the process of production and have no recoverable value. Waste occurs invisibly in the form of evaporation or shrinkage and be visible and solid as well. Examples of visible wastes are gases, dust, valueless residue. Sometimes disposal of waste entails additional expenditure. Example- atomic waste. Loss in the form of waste increases the cost of production.

ACCOUNTING TREATMENT FOR WASTAGE:

Waste has no value. The accounting treatment differs according to waste being normal or abnormal.

NORMAL WASTE:

absorb

This is the inherent waste while manufacturing. It is in the form of evaporation, deterioration etc. The total cost of normal waste is distributed among the good units of output.

ABNORMAL WASTE:

write P/L
P/L P&L

The abnormal waste is transferred to costing profit and loss account to avoid fluctuation in production cost.

3.5.2 LOSSES THROUGH SCRAP:

Scrap is the residue from certain manufacturing activities that usually have a disposable value. It can also be the discarded materials which could fetch additional income. Examples of scrap

20

are materials from stamping operations, filings, sawdust, short lengths from woodworking operations, sprues and 'flash' from foundry and moulding processes. Scrap may be sold or reused.

ACCOUNTING TREATMENT FOR SCRAP:

SALE VALUE OF SCRAP CREDITED TO PROFIT AND LOSS ACCOUNTS:

The sale value is credited to profit and loss account as other income. The cost of output is inclusive of scrap cost. This method of accounting treatment is adopted when the value is negligible.

THE SALE VALUE CREDITED TO OVERHEAD OR MATERIAL COST:

The sale value is reduced with selling cost of scrap, and the net sale value is deducted from factory overhead or material cost. This method is adopted, when several jobs are done simultaneously and it is not possible to segregate the scraps jobs.

CREDITING THE SALE VALUE TO THE JOB OR PROCESS IN WHICH SCRAP ARISES:

The sale value of scrap is credited to the job or process concerned from which the scrap has arisen. This method is followed when identification of scrap with specific jobs or processes is easy.

3.5.2 LOSSES THROUGH SPOILAGE:

Spoilage occurs when goods are damaged beyond rectification. It is disposed of without further processing. Spoilage cost is the cost up to the point of rejection less sale value.

The method of sale of spoilage depends on the extent of spoilage. Some of the spoilage is sold as second grade if the extent of damage is less and the rest may be sold as scrap or treated as waste.

ACCOUNTING TREATMENT OF SPOILAGE:

Accounting treatment depends on whether the spoilage is normal or abnormal. Normal spoilage is borne by good units of output since it is inherent with production and happens even under efficient conditions. However, an abnormal spoilage is avoidable under efficient conditions. The cost of abnormal spoilage is charged to profit and loss account and not to the cost of goods sold.

3.5.3 LOSSES THROUGH DEFECTIVES:

It is a part of production which can be rectified and made into good units with additional cost. The defective work occurs due to raw materials of inferior quality being used, bad planning and poor workmanship. Defective units are rectified with additional cost of material, labour and overheads, and sold as 'first quality' or 'seconds'.

ACCOUNTING TREATMENT OF DEFECTIVES:

The accounting treatment depends on the extent of defectives production. If it is normal being inherent with production, it is identified with specific jobs. The cost of rectification is charged to specific jobs. If the cost is not traced with a job, the cost of rectification is treated as factory overhead.

If the defective work is out of abnormal circumstances, the cost of the rectification is transferred to profit and loss account.

3.6 PRIMARY PACKING MATERIALS COST:

The cost of primary packing material used for a product shall form part of the cost of production. These packaging materials

are essential to hold the product and bring it to a condition in which it can be used by or sold to customers. Primary packing materials are of various types, and their use varies with industry to industry, such as the following:

a) Packing Materials are materials used to hold, identify, describe, store, protect, display, transport, promote and make the product marketable and communicate with the consumer.

b) Defectives are packing materials that do not meet quality standards, i.e. reworks or rejects).

c) Reusable Packing Material are materials that are used more than once to pack the product.

d) Scrap are discarded packing material having some value in a few cases and which is usually either disposed of without further treatment or reintroduced into the production of packing material.

Packing Material Development Cost are cost of evaluation of packing material, such as pilot test, field test, consumer research, feedback, and final evaluation cost).

3.7 SECONDARY PACKING MATERIALS COST:

The cost of secondary packing materials are generally to be treated as distribution overhead as these are used to make the product marketable (i.e. cardboard boxes for holding packed cloth, cartons containing packs of biscuits, cartons holding strips of tablets and cardboard boxes used for holding cartons, fancy packing material to attract customers, product literature to inform the customers).

Secondary Packing Material enables the storage, transport, inform customer, promote and otherwise helps to make the product marketable.

CHAPTER 4

DIRECT LABOUR AND BENEFITS

A direct Labour and Benefits standard should be developed using a single labour standard.

DEFINITION:

The cost of production labour and benefits (wages, overtime, shift premium, vacation pay, breaks, meetings, training, downtime, unemployment taxes, paid sick leave, pension or retirement benefits, social taxes, 13th month pay, cost of living adjustments, life and health insurance, employer's match to any employee savings account, retiree medical currently being earned, etc.) required to produce the forecasted volumes using standard labour hours.

Benefits costs for this calculation should not include those expenses normally included in the general services allocation.

the advisory firm

the advisory firm

Exhibit 4.1: Direct Labour Standard Cost

Product	Direct Labour/ Hr	Direct Labour/Rate	Direct Labour /Unit
Product 1	1,5	19,90 €	29,85 €
Product 2	2	6,00 €	12,00 €
Product 3	2	8,00 €	16,00 €
Product 4	2	10,00 €	20,00 €
Total	8	43,90 €	77,85 €

A general service department is a cost centre that provides services to the rest of an organisation. The manager of a service department is responsible for ensuring that costs are kept down, or to ensure that costs are kept to a minimum as stated in the budget. The services provided by a service department are allocated to the other departments of a business that use these services.

The following are some of the examples of service departments:

Exhibit 4.2: General Service Allocation

Maintenance Department	Charges the production department for labour and equipment consumed during the maintenance of machinery, accumulated by individual machine maintenance job.
Property Caretaker	This could include charges for cleaning services or building maintenance work based on square footage basis.
Purchasing Department	Charges for its efforts in purchasing of goods/services. The allocation may be based on total amount purchased or the number of POs 'placed.
IT Department	Charges other departments for the use of IT storage, bandwidth, by user, or other reasonable method of allocation.
Accounting Department	Some costs can be considered as service department, since payments to suppliers can be traced back to the ordering departments, and customer billings are related to customer-specific profitability tracking.

Direct labour is the product of the direct labour rate times (∗) the standard labour hours required to complete the manufacturing process.

A standard labour hour will include all the following:

- Production labour requirements for direct manufacturing
- Setup
- Line supply
- Line Maintenance and Electricians
- Relief Help
- Contract Substitutes, etc., but excludes exempt business team support
- Palletizing
- Materials and distribution warehouse personnel costs.

All labour that is required for production should be included in the labour standard, including (fractionally) shared personnel or those employees that normally support more than one line or production area.

4.1 DIRECT LABOUR RATE:

The direct labour rate is the total production labour and benefits cost divided by the number of labour hours available for the period.

In some countries like Germany, direct labour rates per hour will be set by reference to the payroll and any agreements on pay rises with the trade union representatives of the employees. A separate hourly rate or weekly wage will be set for each different labour grade/type of employee and an average hourly rate with be applied for each grade (even though individual rates of pay may vary according to experience).

For example, if the July-December cost of production labour and benefits is expected to be as follows:

Direct Labour Rate
Labour Hrs
Ordinary Time   €405.000
Overtime Basic Wage   €95.000
                              €500.000
                              25.000 Hrs

Standard Costs of Direct Labour €20/per Hour.

4.2 INDIRECT LABOUR COSTS CLASSIFICATION:

These are labour costs or wages that are not charged directly to a product. They're wages of non-productive personnel in the production department, e.g. foremen. And are classified as indirect labour costs: overtime premium, shift allowance, bonus payment, sick pay, idle time. It means that they'll be debited to the production overhead account.

4.3 FINISHED GOOD LABOUR STANDARD:

For Manufacturing/Processing:

In this process, you'll multiply the standard labour hours per pound/kilo times (*) the direct labour rate to determine the direct labour cost per pound/kilo.

Cost per case - Multiply the standard pound/kilos of formula required per finished good case * the direct labour cost per pound/kilo to determine the direct labour cost per case.

For Filling/Assembly:

Here, you will multiply the standard labour hours per case/unit times (*) the direct labour rate to determine the direct labour cost per case.

Note: if significant wage variances exist between production areas or technologies, separate direct labour rates should be calculated or a review of the way labour costs are recorded.

4.4 REVIEW OF LABOUR COSTS RECORDING:

The labour attendance time: this should be recorded on, for example, an attendance record or clock card.

Job time: may be recorded on daily timesheet, weekly timesheets or on a job card, depending on the circumstances. Do remember that the manual recording of times on timesheets or job cards is, however, liable to error or even deliberate manipulation and may be unreliable.

The labour cost of pieceworkers should be recorded on a piecework ticket/operation card or electronically.

CHAPTER 5

MANUFACTURING PROCESSING & FILLING/ASSEMBLY

---
o

DEFINITION:

These are expenses that are associated with the area used by the manufacturing/processing and filling/assembly processes. This is the so-called "User Fee" for utilising the equipment and area to manufacture, process, fill, or assemble a product. The cost centre charge includes the following expenses:

- Depreciation of manufacturing/processing or filling/assembly equipment in the cost centre.

- Occupancy expenses for the "space costs" of the manufacturing/processing or filling/assembly area used, allocated on the basis of square meters occupied. Occupancy costs include building depreciation and taxes, heating costs, building repairs, ventilation equipment, etc.

- Supplies expenses for the manufacturing/processing or filling/assembly area used. This includes glue, tape, cleaning supplies, lubricants, eye protectors, uniforms, gloves, etc. used in production, setup, and housekeeping.

- Waste Removal expenses for removal or recycling of regular production scrap material from the cost centre.

- Utilities expenses for electricity, gas, water, sewage, oil, air, etc. that can be estimated or measured in the cost centre. It does not include utilities for heating and cooling that are included in the occupancy allocation, or propellant directly used in products (i.e., for gas house use).

Repairs & Maintenance: In-house, central, and contractor costs to repair and maintain equipment (including the cost of fully allocated labour and replacement parts or materials) in the cost centre.

Other Costs: other expenses associated with the operation of the cost centre (equipment rentals, equipment taxes, cleaning services, etc.).

5.1 COST CENTRE RATE:

For Manufacturing/Processing Area:

It might better to combine all anticipated cost centre expenses for the period to determine the total operating cost. Determine the number of standard labour/machine hours required in the cost centre by multiplying the standard labour/machine hour requirements for each work-in-process/intermediate times (*) the anticipated work-in-process/intermediate volumes for the period. The total anticipated cost centre operating expenses for the period are divided by the projected standard labour/machine hours to arrive at an estimated cost per standard labour/machine hour.

Exhibit 5.1 Cost Centre Rate Manufacturing/Processing

Description	A Car system Mass "kg"	Average Cost/" € /kg"	Hrs/kg	Salary
Body Structure Subsystem			3	82.000 €
Underbody Assy	64,95	0,85 €	22	
Front Structure Assy	44,07	0,41 €	15	
Roof Assy	55,67	0,28 €	19	
Bodyside Assy	137,63	1,40 €	46	
Ladder Assy	93,56	0,14 €	31	
Bolt on BIP Components	0,77	33,93 €	0	
Body Closure Subsystem				109.400 €
Hood Assy	59,54	0,70 €	20	
Front Door Assy	0,00	0,00 €	0	
Rear Door Assy	56,44	0,56 €	19	
Rear Hatch Assy	0,00	0,00 €	0	
Front Fenders	16,24	1,43 €	5	

Bumpers Subsystem				125.072 €
Front Bumper Assy	0,00	0,00 €	0	
Rear Bumper Assy	0,00	0,00 €	0	
Total	528,88	39,69 €	176	316.472 €

Cost Centre Rate/Standard Hour
(H19/G19)   1.795 €
For Filling/Assembly Area:

For Filling/Assembly Area:

Maybe you might want to combine all anticipated cost centre expenses for the period to determine the total operating cost. Determine the number of standard labour/machine hours required in the cost centre by multiplying the standard labour/machine hour requirements for each product times (*) the anticipated volume for the period. The total anticipated cost centre expenses for the period are divided (/) by the projected standard labour/machine hours to arrive at an estimated cost per standard labour/machine hour.

Note: It is also important to note that there is a distinction between machine hours and run hours. For example, 3 machines operating for 8 hours each equals 24 machine hours and 8 run hours.

I have included labour hour in this section, to allocate Manufacturing/Processing and Filling/Assembly costs, though, machine hours should be used.

5.2 FINISHED GOOD LABOUR STANDARD:

For Manufacturing/Processing:

Multiply the number of pound/kilos of formula required per finished goods case/unit times (*) the standard machine-hours required per pound/kilo times (*) the cost per standard machine hour to determine the manufacturing/processing cost centre expense per case/unit.

For Filling/Assembly:

Multiply the number of standard machine-hours required per finished good case/unit times (*) the estimated cost per standard machine hour to determine the filling/assembly cost centre expense per case/unit.

Exhibit 5.2 Cost Centre Rate Filling/Assembly

Description	A Car system Mass "kg"	Average Cost/"€/kg"	Hrs/kg	Salary	Other Overhead Costs
Body Structure Subsystem			2,5	82,000 €	
Underbody Assy	64,95	0,85 €	24		
Front Structure Assy	44,07	0,41 €	16		
Roof Assy	55,67	0,28 €	21		
Bodyside Assy	137,63	1,40 €	51		
Ladder Assy	93,56	0,14 €	35		
Bolt on BIP Components	0,77	33,93 €	0		
Body Closure Subsystem				109,400 €	
Hood Assy	59,54	0,70 €	22		

Front Door Assy	0,00	0,00 €	10		
Rear Door Assy	56,44	0,56 €	21		
Rear Hatch Assy	0,00	0,00 €	0		
Front Fenders	16,24	1,43 €	15		
Bumpers Subsystem				125,072 €	
Front Bumper Assy	0,00	0,00 €	0		
Rear Bumper Assy	0,00	0,00 €	0		
Total	528,88	39,69 €	215	316,472 €	120,000 €

CHAPTER 6

HUMAN RESOURCES BURDEN

DEFINITION:

This is the allocation of general services and human resources expenses to factory labour and the staff cost centre.

Human Resources:

The salary, benefits and expenses of all human resources personnel that support the manufacturing operation or it's services groups (a fractional personnel allocation can also be made, if necessary). For purposes of calculating Human Resources Burden, costs of the payroll function should be excluded.

General Services:

It is the proportional share based on headcount of shared personnel services provided by the company. These shared services include a medical centre, cafeteria, office services, benefits management, company store, etc.

6.1 HUMAN RESOURCES BURDEN RATE:

To determine the total salary, wage, and benefit-cost for all factory labour and factory staff support positions for the period. Divide (/) the total human resources burden expense by the total salary, wage, and benefits cost for factory and factory support positions to determine a human resources burden % ratio. Allocate human resources burden to all production and service cost centres, using the human resources burden % ratio times (*) total salaries, wages, and benefits in each cost centre.

Exhibit 6.1 Human Resources Burden Rate

HR-Burden Rate					
Total Human Resources Burden Expense	20.13 1 €				
Total Factory & Factory Support Salary + Wages+ Benefits Expenses	112.1 61 €				
Absorption Rate	20.13 1 €	X	100	17,9%	
	Basis of Appor t	Production		Service	Total

	Proces sing	Fillin g	Assemb ly	Stores	
Production & Service Cost	29,50 0 €	32,42 1 €	31,159 €	19,081 €	112,1 61 €
HR Burden 17,9% Rate	5,295 €	5.819 €	5.592 €	3.425 €	20.13 1 €
Total	34,79 5 €	38,24 0 €	36,751 €	22,505 €	132,2 91 €

6.2 FINISHED GOOD STANDARD:

Use the human resources % ratio times (*) salaries and benefits in manufacturing support departments to allocate human resources cost to all support departments. For production costs. Use the human resources burden % ratio times (*) the direct labour cost per case/unit to determine the human resources burden cost per case/unit.

CHAPTER 7

STOCK KEEPING UNIT (SKU)/VOLUME RELATED BURDEN

DEFINITION:

- These are the expenses of plant operations management and supporting staff. The expense includes the following:

- Plant Management: They're the expenses of the factory manager and all related staff that manage the business teams. If business teams are not used, the expenses of business teams noted below will be included in the plant management total.

- Business Teams: The expenses include planning, purchasing, engineering, and the team facilitator functions that directly support the operations and any other service cost centres that support production operations should be included as well.

- Quality Assurance: The expenses of the quality assurance function, include the supplier qualification and certification.

- Purchasing Team: The expenses of purchasing team should be included.

- Research & Development or Manufacturing Support Team: The expenses of research and development is devoted to manufacturing support only. This includes process development, package qualification, and materials qualification.

- Finance: It's the financial support group that services the manufacturing unit. This includes financial support for expense budgeting in manufacturing, product costing, new product support, and accounts payable for factory suppliers. If this function is only a portion of several combined responsibilities for a person or group, a fractional estimate of the total cost should be used.

- IT/IS: These are expenses of systems and programming personnel or contractors that directly support manufacturing operations. Does not include computer usage transfers, which should be directly transferred to the user departments.

Note: SKU/volume burden related to purchased finished goods/contract labour is (referred in section entitled "Purchased Finished Goods, Contract Labour" below). For allocation purposes, it requires specific separation.

7.1 SKU/VOLUME RELATED BURDEN RATE:

It is best to consolidate total SKU/Volume-related burden expenses to determine the total for the period. Divide (/) the SKU/Volume burden expenses by the estimated number of production runs for the period to determine the cost per production run. If production runs are not a measure used (i.e., for continuous production or purchased items) estimated purchase orders can be substituted for this measure.

7.2 FINISHED GOOD STANDARD:

To calculate the finished goods standard, you'll have to combine finished goods SKU's into common manufacturing units, though, only SKU's that share a common formula, container (i.e., can or bottle), and closure (i.e., cap or trigger) and are regularly scheduled together for production (not necessarily on the same production order) are considered common manufacturing units (CMU's). Variation should only exist in label (including a pouch and shipping carton.

It is advisable to try and sort common manufacturing units from highest to lowest volume, and group them into quartiles (ABCD, with "A" the top 25% of the total CMU volume). Sum the total number of anticipated production runs in each quartile (planned average run length can be used to estimate the number of production runs). Allocate the production run costs noted above to each quartile (ABCD) by multiplying (*) the total number of anticipated production runs in each quartile times (*) the cost per production run.

Determine the cost per case by dividing (/) the total quartile production run cost by the case (physical cases, not stat cases) volume in the quartile to get the rate per case. This common rate per case should be allocated to all products in the quartile. As a reminder, physical cases are the basis for this allocation regardless of the number of units per case.

Exhibit 7.1 SKU Volume Related Burden

SKU/Volume Related Burden							
Plant Management	Business Teams	Quality Assurance	Purchasing Team	R&D	Finance	IT/IS	total SKU/Volume-related burden expenses
49,000 €	31,220 €	19,500 €	22,125 €	39,687 €	32,750 €	22.000 €	216,282 €
No. Unit Sold per Month	1.000	Unit					
No. Production Run	12.000	Unit					

(12 months)								
Make to Stock (Sales Forecast)	1.000	Month						
Total SKU/Volume-related burden expenses	216.282							
Cost /Production Run	18 €	€216.282/ 12.000						

CHAPTER 8

MATERIAL WAREHOUSE BURDEN

DEFINITION:

This is to do with all the expenses that are associated with receiving and storage of raw materials and packaging materials into the warehouse before production but does not include cost of line supply personnel that are part of indirect labour. However, if the cost is significant and meaningful (i.e., no less than 20% of the time in any one area), personnel expenses for individuals performing both line supply and material receiving and storage can be split between direct labour and warehouse burden based on the proportion of time spent on each function.

Materials warehouse burden includes the cost of materials warehouse personnel, equipment rental or depreciation, equipment repair, warehouse occupancy, outside storage costs, and freight to and from outside storage. If the materials and finished goods warehouse are shared, use the average proportion of total warehouse space, the materials area occupies to determine the allocation of total warehouse expenses to the materials warehouse.

Palletiser labour and overhead expenses should be excluded from the cost of sales, as they are treated as distribution expenses.

Note: A Palletiser is a machine which provides an automatic means for stacking cases of goods or products onto a pallet.

8.1 MATERIALS WAREHAUSE BURDEN RATE:

At this point, we ought to consolidate all materials warehouse expenses and divide it (/) by anticipating physical cases/units of production to determine a common cost per case/unit.

Exhibit 8.1 Materials Warehouse Burden Rate

Material Warehouse Burden Rate				
Description	Monthly	Raw Mat. Sq.	Finished Goods Sq.	Sq
Warehouse Personnel & Fringe Benefits	11.500,00 €	400	800%	1200
Warehouse Equipment Rental	800,00 €			
Depreciation.	1.100,00 €			
Equipment Repair	536,00 €			
Wahrehouse Rent	1.892,00 €			
External Warehouse Storage Location (NL)	755,00 €			
Freight cost from/to 3rd-Party Warehouse Facility (Ave.)	439,00 €			
Total Cost	17.022,00 €			
Production Unit / month (run)	1.000			
Cost per Unit	17,02 €			

CHAPTER 9

PRODUCTION PRIME AND CONVERSION COST

In this chapter, I am not envisioning to go into great detail, as I would have assumed that you would have mastered the various calculation method. Instead, I am merely using it demonstration and to jog your memory.

As you know, developing standards is not a simple task, as it requires a lot of judgment and practical experience in identifying the kind of materials, labour types, quantities, and prices as well as understanding the behavioural elements of the organisational overhead. Hence, we'll need to estimate unit cost for each cost element (standard resource price and standard resource usage/quantity.

9.1 SETTING RAW MATERIAL STANDARDS:

The first step in setting the material standards is to identify and list those specific direct materials which are to be used, in making the product. This list is often available on the product specification documents that have been prepared by the engineering department. In the absence of such documentation, the material specifications can be determined by observing the production area, enquiring of production personnel, inspecting material requisitions, or reviewing past cost accounts related to the product. Three key areas ought to be observed, in terms of the material inputs, and that's as follows:

- Types of inputs
- Quantity of inputs used, and
- Quality of inputs used

Exhibit 9.1: Direct Material

Standard Cost Card			
Company: Product:	Cable GmbH XY		
Direct Material	Cost	Requirement	Euro
Component 1	€3,00 per m	4,4 metres	13,20 €
Component 2	€5,00 per m	6,0 metres	30,00 €
Direct Material Cost			43,20 €

9.2 SETTING DIRECT LABOUR STANDARD:

In today's manufacturing industry, the direct labour cost accounts for the most considerable expense of manufacturing products, which is why it's essential to keep track of the company's labour cost per unit, to ensure that wages are not growing faster than company's profits. Although, in some industries, this may signal demand for that particular industry products are growing.

In terms of setting direct labour standard, there is no difference to those of direct material, as they share the same basic approach. Some production companies use a mixture of employees and machines or one of those. It's still important to separate the two when time standards are used. Setting the functional standards, quantitative data for each production operation has to be obtained, possibly from the industrial engineering studies, accounting system and estimates from those who are involved in the manufacturing process. Although there is an alternative method in setting a time standard, it is the average time that was used to manufacture a product during the past year. Such information can be obtained from employees' past timesheets. However, the risk factor that is attached is that some of the historical information might contain some inefficiencies or might not contain all useful information.

Exhibit 9.2: Direct Labour

Standard Cost Card			
Company:	Cable GmbH		
Product:	XY		
Direct Labour	Cost	Requirement	Euro
Grade II	€22.75 per hour	3.0 hours	68.25
Grade III	€15.25 per hour	4.0 hours	61.00
Total Standard Cost			129.25

9.3 SETTING OVERHEAD STANDARD:

Overhead standards are simply the predetermined factory overhead application rates. It is the cost incurred in the course of making a product, providing a service or running a department, but which cannot be traced directly and in full to the product, service or department. Overhead is the total of the following:

- Indirect materials
- Indirect Labour
- Indirect Expenses

To provide the most appropriate costing information for overhead, you would have to calculate the overhead absorption rates using the estimated budget figure for next year, using this 4-steps approach, as shown below:

- Step 1: Estimate the overhead likely to be incurred during the coming year, for example Euro 1.200.000.

- Step 2: Estimate the activity level for the coming year; for example, the manufacturing company have budgeted an activity level of 100.000 units for the budgeted year.

- Step 3: Divide the estimated overhead by the budgeted activity level, Euro 1.200.000/100.000 = Euro 12.

- Step 4: Now, apply the manufacturing overhead to the goods produced using Euro 12,00 as your standard overhead absorption rate.

Exhibit 9.3: Overhead

Standard Cost Card			
Company: Product:	Cable GmbH XY		
Factory Overheads	Cost	Requirement	Euro
Variable Overhead	€1,50/per hour	5.0 hours	7,50 €
Fixed Overhead	€2,50/per hour	5 hours	12,50 €
Total Overhead			20,00 €

Data from the standard cost card are used to assign costs to inventory accounts (Raw Material, WIP and Finished Goods), and actual and standard costs, are recorded in a standard cost system. It is always worth remembering that it is only the standard rather than actual costs of production, are debited to Work-in-Process (WIP) Inventory, and any difference between the actual and a standard cost is called a variance.

9.4 COST ACCUMULATION AND COST ACCOUNTING

What's cost accumulation? Cost accumulation can be defined, as a process of collecting costs in an organised manner using cost accounting system. In this cost accounting system, there are two primary approaches to cost accumulation, and they're absorption costing and marginal costing.

9.5 ABSORPTION COSTING

Absorption costing cost accumulation system is the traditional method of product costing which aims to include in the total cost of a product, an appropriate share of a company's total overhead so to reflects the amount of time and effort that has gone into producing the product. It is used in dealing with overheads, which involves three stages of allocation, apportionment, and absorption.

1st-STEP COST ALLOCATION:

The cost allocation is a process in which the entire costs of an item are charged directly to the cost units or departments, i.e. assembly, packaging, and quality control) either direct or indirect. Direct costs are allocated directly to the cost units. Indirect or Overhead costs of all factory activities are collected in one cost pool and allocate those costs from the cost pool to each product, using one predetermined overhead rate.

2ⁿᵈ-STEP APPORTIONMENT:

The cost apportionment is used to apportion overhead to departments or cost centres. There are two stages in the process, and they're the general overhead apportionment and the service department cost apportionment.

i.   General overheads apportionment

The costs aren't allocated directly to a specific cost centre or department, manufacturing, finishing or service (e.g. electricity, repairs, depreciation, rent, staff canteen, staff training. For example, the insurance cost for the premises cannot be directly allocated to one department and is, therefore, included in the general overheads, which are later apportioned between various departments. The overhead cost is then apportioned using the following formula for each base:

- Apportionment = Overhead cost x Department base quantity / Total base quantity

ii.   Service department cost apportionment

There are also various methods of service department cost apportionment, such as direct and repeated distribution method. So that after apportionment, overheads are absorbed into products using an appropriate absorption rate based on budgeted costs and budgeted volume of activities.

There are three methods for allocating service department costs:

- The first method, the direct method, is the simplest of the three. The direct method allocates the costs of each of the service departments to each operating department based on each department's share of the allocation base. Services used by other service departments are ignored.

- The second method of allocating the service department's cost is the step method. The method allocates costs to the operating departments and other service departments in a sequential process. The sequence of allocation generally starts with the service department that has incurred the most followed by the next service department and so forth until the service department with the lowest costs has had its costs allocated. No costs are re-allocated back to a department that has already had all of its costs allocated.

- The third method is the most complicated, as well as the most accurate. The reciprocal method allocates services department costs to operating departments and other service departments. Then under this method, the relationship between service departments is recognised. And cost is allocated to, and from each service department for services provided.

3rd-STEP ABSORPTION:

Absorption is the final stage of the process of absorbing overhead costs into a product, which have been allocated and apportioned to the production cost centres.

The under-/over-absorbed overhead is a word that most people who work in the finance departments have to deal with at least, every month-end close when they've to analysis the actual production costs. Under-/over-absorbed overhead occurs, when overheads incurred during the month deviates from the overhead absorbed, this is because the overhead absorbed is based on an estimated expenditure and activity level.

9.6 MARGINAL COSTING

Marginal costing is the cost of producing an additional unit of output. The method is different from the traditional absorption costing. Because, it uses only variable costs to value inventory, which means that fixed costs are treated as periodic costs and charged in full against the period that they were incurred.

Contribution is used in place of gross profit. It's the difference between sales revenue and variable (marginal) costs of sales.

Inventory is valued at variable production cost, i.e. it doesn't include full production costs as with absorption costing. Even some companies use the concept of marginal costing in their production to determine the optimum production quantity.

Marginal costing will show how the cash flow and profit is affected by the changes in sales volumes since contribution varies in direct proportion to units sold.

Exhibit 9.4: Example of an exercise using Standard Cost Card for the Absorption Costing and Marginal Costing.

For example, CH GmbH budgets to produce and sell 3.600 units of its product during 20X8 at a selling price of €5,50 per unit. Production variable costs are €3,00 per unit and fixed costs for the year were budgeted at €6.000 (divisible equally between the 12 months of the year).

Sales demand in the first half of the year is expected to be only 200 units per month, but monthly demand will double in the second half of the year. To save unnecessary production costs, the company has budgeted to spread production evenly over the year. Though, the actual costs were 4.80 Euro/piece.

9.7 EXAMPLES OF USING ABSORPTION AND MARGINAL COSTING

Let us calculate the profits for each month using the following costing methods:

- Absorption costing

- Marginal costing

ABSORPTION COSTING

The fixed overhead absorption rate is €6.000 / 3.600 = €1,67 (from Exhibit 9.4)

Example of the first six months of the year, profit per month would be as follows:

Exhibit 9.5: Exercise using Standard Cost Card for the Absorption Costing.

	€
Sales (200 units x €5,50)	1.100,00
Less full cost of sales (200 x €4,67)	934,00
	166,00
Under-/over-absorbed overhead (200 x €0,09 (4,67€ - 4,58))	-18,00
Profit (€0,74 per unit)	148,00

For each of the second six months of the year, profit per month would be as follows;

Exhibit 10.6: Exercise using Standard Cost Card for the

Absorption Costing

	€
Sales (400 units x €5,50)	2.200,00
Less full cost of sales (400 x €4,67)	1.868,00
	332,00
Under-/over-absorbed overhead (400 x €0,09)	-36,00
Profit (€0,74 per unit)	296,00

MARGINAL COSTING

For each of the first six months of the year.

Exhibit 9.7: Example of an exercise using Standard Cost Card for the Marginal Costing.

For each of the second six months of the year, profit per month

	€
Sales (200 units x €5,50)	1.100,00
Less variable cost of sales (200 x €3,00)	600,00
Contribution (€2,50 per unit)	500,00
Less fixed costs (1,67€)	334,00
Profit (€0,83 per unit)	166,00

would be as follows:

Exhibit 9.8: Exercise using Standard Cost Card for the Marginal

Costing.

	€
Sales (400 units x €5,50)	2.200,00
Less variable cost of sales (400 x €3,00)	1.200,00
Contribution (€2,50 per unit)	1.000,00
Less fixed costs (1,67€)	668,00
Profit (€0,82 per unit)	332,00

9.8 BENEFITS OF ADOPTING AND MAINTAINING STANDARD COST STYSTEM

- Standard costs provide a basis for sensible cost comparisons.

- Standard costs enable cost accountants, management accountants and controllers to compute the allowed standard cost, given actual output, which serves as a yardstick to compare with the actual cost incurred. This computation of standard costs enables managers to apply management by exception for their teams.

- The use of standard costs in product costing results in more stable product costs than if actual production costs were used.

- The use of standard-costing system could be less expensive than an actual- or normal-costing system.

- To adhere to standards could help to motivate employees, where rewards are offered for excellent performance.

ANALYSING VARIANCE

CHAPTER 10

VARIANCE ANALYSIS

DEFINITION:

Variance is defined as the difference between a planned, budgeted, or standard cost and the actual cost incurred. This difference between standard and actual result is analysed, and it's known as the variance analysis. Then, if the actual result is better than expected result, it's known as a favourable variance (F), however, if the result is worse than expected, it's known as an adverse variance (A).

When variances occur in a standard, most companies investigate it to determine the causes, so that the necessary action would be taken, to perform better next time. In other words, variance analysis is a process of identifying causes of variation in the cost of goods sold, profit and loss of the month or budget, and it helps to understand why fluctuations happened and what can or should be done to reduce the adverse variance. It's also a yardstick in which to measure performance.

In management accounting, there are two types of standards which are used to analyse variances.

10.1 VARIANCE ANALYSIS COMPONENTS

Variances are excellent devices for measuring operating performance, at the same time, cost accountants or controller should investigate, to ensure they understand the reasons for the deviation. Secondly, as a variance analysis is used to isolate deviations quickly and correct, and as a rule of thumb, it's best to set up a value to which a deviation limit is laid down, for example, Euro 5.000 so that any value below the agreed amount is considered immaterial.

Below are examples of the different kinds of actual and standard outcome:

Favourable   Actual Cost < Standard
Favourable   Actual Revenue > Standard
Unfavourable/Adverse   Actual Cost > Standard
Unfavourable/Adverse   Actual Revenue < Standard

Exhibit 10.1: All costs have two components, volume and rate, as shown below:

Costs =	Volume Component X	Rate Component
Raw Material Cost =	Quantity purchased X	Cost per unit
Raw Material Used =	Quantity used X	Cost per unit
Direct Labour Cost =	DL Hours X	Hourly Rate
Overhead Cost =	Cost Driver X	Burden Rate

10.2 DIRECT MATERIAL:

According to experts, it's recommended that the starting point when analysing variances should be the material variance analysis. Material variance analysis is the difference between actual costs and standard (or budgeted) costs and it's typically explained by three separate variances:

- Direct Material total variance
- Direct Materials price variance

- Direct Materials quantity variance

The total material variance is the difference between what the output actually costed and what it should have costed in in terms of material. This variance is divided into the following sub-variances:

- The materials price variance is the difference between what the material did cost and what it should have cost
- The materials quantity variance is the difference between the standard cost of the material that should have been used and the standard cost of the material that was used

Exhibit 10.2: Direct Material Total Variance

Company CH GmbH produces product T at a standard direct material cost of 10 kilograms of material Z at Euro 10 per kilogram (€100,00 per unit T). During the year, 1.000 units of T were manufactured, using 12.000 kilograms of material Z which cost Euro 99.800.

The material total material variance is the difference between what 1.000 units should have costed and what they did cost.

Material Total Variance		
	Euro	
1.000 Units Should Have Cost (10kg x €10)	100,000,00	
But did cost	99,800,00	
Material Total Variance		€ 200 (F)

The variance is favourable because the units' cost is less than they should have costed.

10.2.1 DIRECT MATERIAL PRICE VARIANCE:

It's the difference between the actual price and standard price:

Equation: Material Price Variance = $(AQ \times AP) - (AQ \times SP)$

(Actual Quantity x Actual Price) - (Actual Quantity x Standard Price) Or

$(AP - SP) \times AQP$

(Actual Price – Standard Price) x Actual Quantity.

Exhibit 11.3: Direct Material Price Variance

Company CH GmbH produces product T at a standard direct material cost of 10 kilograms of material Z at Euro 10 per kilogram (€100,00 per unit T). During the year, 1.000 units of T were manufactured, using 12.000 kilograms of material Z which cost Euro 99.800.

The materials price variance is the difference between what 12.000 kgs should have cost, and 12.000 kgs did cost.

Direct Material Price Variance		
	Euro	
12.000 kgs Z should have cost (x €10)	120.000	
But did cost	99.800	
Material Z Price Variance		€ 20.200 (F)

The variance is favourable because the material cost less than it should have.

10.2.2 REASONS FOR DIRECT MATERIAL PRICE VARIANCE:

The following are some of the factors that might cause direct material price variances:

- Buying materials that are of different quality than that planned in the standard material cost
- Using old standard cost per unit of raw material that are no longer applicable by suppliers
- Buying of raw materials were performed through a new supplier, whose delivery terms for purchases were different, i.e. either more or less expensive than the terms used when standard material costs were set in the systems.
- Buying manager might have been in a rush when he was ordering the raw materials, thereby, buying the wrong

quantity of materials and differed norms (e.g., larger lot sizes which would yield quantity discounts).

10.2.3 DIRECT MATERIAL QUALITY VARIANCE:

- It's the difference between actual quantity and standard quantity.
- Equation: Materials quantity variance = (AQ × SP) – (SQ × SP.
- (Actual Quantity x Standard Price) – (Standard Quantity x Standard Price).

Exhibit 10.4: Direct Material Quantity Variance

Company CH GmbH produces product T at a standard direct material cost of 10 kilograms of material Z at Euro 10 per kilogram (€100,00 per unit T). During the year, 1.000 units of T were manufactured, using 12.000 kilograms of material Z which cost Euro 99.800.

The materials quantity variance is the difference between how many kilograms of Z should have been used to produce 1.000 units of T and how many kilograms were used, valued at the standard cost of the material that should have been used and the standard cost per kilogram.

Direct Material Quantity Variance		
	Kgs	
1.000 units T should have used (x 10kgs)	10.000	
But did use	12.000	
Material Quantity Variance in Kgs		2.000 (A)
X standard cost per kilogram	X	10,00 €
Material Quantity Variance in Euro		20.000 (A)

The variance is adverse because more material than should have been used was used.

Exhibit 10.5: Summary Direct Material Variance

Summary
Price Variance   €20.200 (F)
Usage Variance   €-20.000 (A)
Total Variance   € 200 (F)

10.2.4 REASONS FOR DIRECT MATERIAL QUANTITY VARIANCE:

The following are some of the factors that might cause direct material quantity variances:

- Probably, the employees were poorly supervised during their shifts.

- There has been inefficient maintenance of machinery and equipment which might have caused numerous machine break downs.

- Out of date materials were used in setting direct material quantity.

- It might be that the production manager used different direct materials quantity, instead of the standard quantities.

10.3. DIRECT LABOUR VARIANCE:

The direct labour (DL) variance is the difference between the standard cost for actual production and the actual cost in production. There are three sub-categories, as shown below:

- Total direct labour variance
- Direct labour rate variance
- Direct labour efficiency (productivity) variance

Total Labour Variance

The total labour variance is the difference between what the output should have costed and what it did cost, in terms of labour, and its sub-divided into two sub-variances. A useful control mechanism for businesses because it gives insight into how much of the production costs goes towards production employees.

Exhibit 10.6: Direct Labour Total Variance

The standard direct labour cost of product T is 3 hours of unskilled employees worked at €8,50 per hour (€25,50 per unit of T). During the run-up to the year-end, the company manufactured 1.000 units of their product T, and the direct labour cost of the unskilled labour used was €22.695 for 2.500 hours of work.

The labour total variance is the difference between what the output should have costed and what it did cost, in terms of labour.

Direct Labour Total Variance		
	Euro	
1.000 units should have cost (3 hrs x €8,50=€25,50)	25,500	
But did cost	22,695	
Labour Total Variance	2,805 (F)	

The variance is favourable because the units cost less than they should have done.

10.3.1 DIRECT LABOUR RATE VARIANCE

The direct labour rate variance is the difference between what the labour did cost and what it should have cost.

Exhibit 10.7: Direct Labour Rate Variance

The standard direct labour cost of product T is 3 hours of unskilled employees worked at €8,50 per hour (€25,50 per unit of T). During the run-up to the year-end, the company manufactured 1.000 units of their product T, and the direct labour cost of the unskilled labour used was €22.695 for 2.500 hours of work.

The labour rate variance is the difference between what 2.500 hours should have cost and what 2.500 hours did cost.

Direct Labour Rate Variance		
	Euro	
2.500 hours should have cost (x €8,50)	21.250	
But did cost	22.695	
Labour Rate Variance		1,445 (A)

The variance is adverse because the units cost more than it should have cost.

10.3.2 DIRECT LABOUR EFFICIENCY (PRODUCTIVITY) VARIANCE

The labour efficiency variance is the difference between the standard cost of the hours that employees should have worked and the standard cost of the hours that the employees worked. It's used to analyse the effectiveness of a business concerning its direct labour.

Exhibit 10.8: Direct Labour Efficiency (Productivity) Variance

The standard direct labour cost of product T is 3 hours of unskilled employees worked at €8,50 per hour (€25,50 per unit of T). During the run-up to the year-end, the company manufactured 1.000 units of their product T, and the direct labour cost of the unskilled labour used was €22.695 for 2.500 hours of work.

The labour efficiency variance is the difference between the number of hours it should have taken to produce 1.000 units of T, and the number of hours it did take, valued at the standard rate per hour.

Direct Labour Efficiency (Prod.) Variance		
	Hours	
1.000 units of T should have taken (x 3 hrs)	3,000	
But did take	2,500	
Labour Efficiency		500 (F)
X standard rate per hour	X	€ 8,50
Efficiency (Productivity) Variance		€ 4,250 (F)

The variance is favourable because less hours were worked than should have been accomplished.

Exhibit 10.9: Summary Direct Labour Variance

Summary

Labour Rate Variance	€ -1.445(A)
Labour Efficiency Variance	€ 4.250 (F)
Total Labour Rate Variance	€ 2.805 (F)

10.3.3 REASON FOR DIRECT LABOUR PRICE VARIANCE:

- It's caused by the use of highly skilled employees, who are paid more money than the unskilled employees.
- The standard labour rate used for unskilled employees could be out of date.
- Overtime worked are included in the direct labour cost, instead of in the manufacturing overhead.
- The changes made in contracts with the union may not have been updated in the standards.

10.3.4 REASON FOR DIRECT LABOUR EFFICIENCY (QUANTITY) VARIANCE:

- It can be caused by using a different mix of labour hours for the task at hand, as compared to the standard mix of labour.
- Cause could be due to inadequate supervision of employees.
- Machinery and equipment aren't properly maintained according to schedules, which could lead to excess wastage and direct labour hour consumption.
- The use of out of date direct labour hour standard when standards were set could cause differences.
- Where morale of the production employees is low, it could lead to sickness.
- Poor production scheduling could lead to excessive idle time.

- The use of newly hired staff in the production could cause an increase in the training period, leading to an increase in labour hours.

10.4 PRODUCTION OVERHEAD VARIANCE

Production overhead is all indirect costs incurred during production processes. This overhead is applied to the units manufactured within a reporting period. Examples of these costs included in the manufacturing overhead category are, salaries purchasing manager, production managers, warehouse managers, quality control manager, material handling management staff.

Production overhead variance is the difference between the actual manufacturing overhead costs incurred and the standard manufacturing overhead costs applied (absorbed) to production using the standard variable and fixed manufacturing overhead rates.

Usually, as the production output increases or decreases, the production variable overhead moves similarly.

For example, if production volume increases say by 10 %, the variable overhead would also increase in close approximation as well. Hence, these costs are apportioned between the goods manufactured in one of the various apportionment methods, mentioned in the earlier chapters.

10.4.1 VARIABLE PRODUCTION OVERHEAD COST VARIANCE:

Variable production overhead total variance is defined as the difference between what the actual output should have costed in terms of the variable costs and what it costs at the end.

The variable production overhead total variance has two separate variance analysis, which are as follows:

Variable Production Overhead Expenditure Variance

Variable Production Overhead Efficiency Variance

10.4.2 VARIABLE PRODUCTION OVERHEAD EXPENDITURE VARIANCE (AKA SPENDING VARIANCE):

It is the difference between the actual variable production overhead incurred and the amount that should have been incurred for the same hours worked, as shown below:

Actual variable overhead	Minus	standard variable overhead
Standard variable overhead	Equals	Actual hours worked multiply by standard rate per hour
Or standard output of actual hours	Multiply by	Standard rate per unit

Exhibit 10.10: Variable Production Overhead Expenditure Variance

NCH GmbH is a first-tier automotive supplier of machines and spare parts. And for one of their production department, the company has set up the following standard variable overhead:

Standard Variable overhead for the period:	€ 18.000
Standard Volume of Production for the period:	2.000 units
Standard time per unit:	1 hours
Standard direct labour rate:	€6,50
Actual variable overheads incurred during the period is	€ 24.000.
Actual production:	2.200 units
Actual hours worked	2.400 hours
Actual direct	€8,00

Variable Overhead Expenditure Variance		
	Euro	
2.400 hours should cost (2.400 x €6,50)	15,600	
But did cost (2.400 x €8,50)	19,200	
Variable Overhead Expenditure Variance	€ 3,600 (A)	

10.4.3 VARIABLE PRODUCTION OVERHEAD EFFICIENCY VARIANCE:

The variable production overhead efficiency variance is the difference between the standard cost of the hours that should have been worked for the number of items produced, and the standard efficiency cost of the actual number of hours worked.

The formula is:

Standard variable overhead rate per hour x (Actual hours – Standard hours of actual production)

Or, Standard rate per unit * (Standard output – Actual output)

Or, Variable overhead recovered – Standard variable overhead.

Exhibit 10.11: Variable Production Overhead Efficiency Variance

NCH GmbH is a first-tier automotive supplier of machines and spare parts. And for one of their production department, the company has set up the following standard variable overhead:

Standard Variable overhead for the period:	€ 18.000
Standard Volume of Production for the period:	2.000 units
Standard time per unit:	1 hours
Standard direct labour rate:	€6,50
Actual variable overheads incurred during the period is	€ 24.000.
Actual production:	2.200 units
Actual hours worked:	2.400 hours
Actual direct:	€8,00

Variable Production Overhead Efficiency Variance		
	Hours	
2.200 units should have taken (2.200 x 1 hours)	2.200	
But did take	2.400	
Variance in hours		200 (A)
X standard rate per hour	X	€ 6,50
Variable Overhead Efficiency Variance		€1.300 A)

Exhibit 10.12: Summary Variable Production Overhead Total Variance

Variable Overhead Expenditure Variance -€3.600 (A)
Variable Overhead Efficiency Variance -€1.300 (A)
Variable Production Overhead Total Variance -€4.900 (A)

10.4.4 REASON FOR VARIABLE EXPENDITURE OVERHEAD VARIANCE:

- Changes in the labour rate could suggest that more skilled employees were deployed or that there was an increase in unskilled employees' wages which weren't updated in the standard cost card. Another reason could be that the unskilled employees may have worked overtime.

- It could be that there was a machine break down, thereby forcing the production workers to have idle time.
- There could be an inefficiency use of the variable overhead.
- Lack of control of an item of overhead cost could have an impact.
- The relationship between variable overheads and direct labour hours weren't adequately defined.

10.4.5 FIXED PRODUCTION OVERHEAD COST VARIANCES:

The fixed production overhead is a fixed cost that remains stable even when there is an increase or decrease in the output. The fixed manufacturing costs, such as rent, depreciation on factory fixed assets, property tax, rent, utility bills are absorbed into the manufactured products through a pre-determined absorption rate. This The fixed production overhead variance is sub-divided into an expenditure variance and a volume (usage) variance. The volume variance is once again subdivided into volume efficiency variance and volume capacity variance.

Exhibit 10.13: Fixed Production Overhead Cost Variances

PanSch GmbH Budget and Actual financial data for their last 4 Months		
Description	Budget	Actual
Sales	1.000.075,20 €	970.072,94 €
Production & Sales Unit	100.000	110.000
COGS:		
Direct Raw Materials	140.110,96 €	135.907,63 €
Direct Labour	149.330,21 €	144.850,30 €
Production Hours	50.000	75.000
Number of Hours per Unit	0,50	0,68
Variable Production Overheads	95.591,81 €	92.724,06 €
Fixed Production Overheads	137.632,00 €	133.503,04 €
Fixed Production Overhead Absorption Rate (FOAR)	2,75 €	1,78 €

Note: The above budget was prepared based on 100.000 units manufactured, and sold. However, the actual number of production and sales units for the four months amounted to 110.000 units.

The company uses absorption costing.

10.4.6 FIXED PRODUCTION OVERHEAD EXPENDITURE VARIANCE

Fixed production overhead expenditure variance is the difference between the budgeted fixed production overhead expenditure and the actual fixed production overhead expenditure during a period.

Exhibit 10.14: Fixed Production Overhead Expenditure Variances

Fixed Production Overhead Expenditure Variance:		
Budgeted Fixed Production Overhead Expenditure	137.632,00 €	
Actual Fixed Production Overhead Expenditure	133.503,04 €	
Fixed Production Overhead Expenditure Variance	4.128,96 €	(F)

The variance is favourable, because we have absorbed more overhead.

101.4.7 FIXED PRODUCTION OVHERHEAD VOLUME VARIANCE

This variance measures the difference between the budgeted and actual production volume or hours and multiplies the difference at the standard fixed overhead absorption rate. In some of the examples, we used some units, rather than labour hours, which was €137.632/100.000 = €1,37 per unit.

Exhibit 10.15: Fixed Production Overhead Volume Variances

Fixed Production Overhead Volume Variance:		
Actual Production at Std. Rate (110.000 x €1,37 per unit)	150.700,00 €	(F)
Budgeted Production at Std. Rate (100.000 x €1,37 per unit)	137.632,00 €	(A)
Fixed Production Overhead Volume Variance	13.068,00 €	(F)

The variance is favourable, because output in volume (110.000 units) were greater than planned.

10.4.8 FIXED PRODUCTION OVERHEAD VOLUME EFFICIENCY VARIANCE

Fixed production overhead volume efficiency variance is the difference between the actual number of hours the production employees spent in making units of product and comparing it to the number of hours it took to make.

Exhibit 10.16: Fixed Production Overhead Volume Efficiency
Variances

Fixed Production Overhead Volume Efficiency Variance:		
110.000 units should have taken (x 0.5 hrs)	55.000	Hours
But did take	75.000	Hours
Fixed Production Overhead Volume Variance in hours	20.000	(A)
x Standard Fixed Production Overhead Absorption Rate per Hour	2,75 €	
Fixed Production Overhead Volume Efficiency Variance:	55.000,00 €	(A)

The variance is unfavourable, because employees were not fast
enough. They have spent 20.000 more than was budgeted.

10.4.9 FIXED PRODUCTION OVERHEAD VOLUME CAPACITY VARIANCE

The fixed production overhead volume capacity variance compares
the number of hours employees have worked to the number of hours
that were budgeted. It will mean that the more hours that were
worked will lead to a greater capacity to produce units.

Exhibit 10.17: Fixed Production Overhead Volume Capacity Variances

Fixed Production Overhead Volume Capacity Variance:	
	Hours
Budgeted Hours of Work	50.000
Actual Hours of Worked	75.000
Fixed Production Overhead Volume Variance in hours	25.000 (F)
x Standard Fixed Production Overhead Absorption Rate per Hour	€2,75
Fixed Production Overhead Volume Capacity Variance:	€68.750(F)

The variance is favourable because the workforce worked 25.000 hours longer than budgeted.

This result shows that more hours have been worked than what was budgeted. This had caused an over-absorption of overhead.

10.5 VARIANCE ANALYSIS CONCLUSION: A MUST-HAVE TOOL

I have seen many companies preferring only to use variance analysis on specific products or parts of the business, thereby not seeing a complete picture of the business. Nonetheless, variance analysis is a must-have controlling tool for any size of an organisation, whether it is by using excel format or any business intelligent software.

Analysing variances especially, during the period close can be a daunting task, at the same time, variance analysis is an essential tool in analysing the mathematical difference between a predetermined cost/income and the actual cost/income, and the appraisal of all aspects of your business dealings.

When used correctly, it could aid in improving the departmental efficiency, by highlighting the activities in need of investigation, especially, the adverse variances.

Variance analysis is used to analyse the inventory valuation which includes all the costs that the business had paid to convert the raw material into its present condition and location so that it's ready for sale to your customers. Thereby, used as a method for controlling inventory so that the business can generate the maximum profit from the least amount of investment made in inventory, at the same time avoiding overstocking and avoiding customer dissatisfaction.

It helps management in setting and evaluation company's objectives.

It assists in decision making, primarily, using marginal costing in pricing strategy, instead of using absorption costing, where all costs are part of the decision-making process.

It can provide a means of performance evaluation and rewards for employees, as such can motivate employees.

Variance analysis can be used to identify the critical success factor of products or business units which would be useful for the survival of a company in a saturated market segment. The use of the variance analysis would highlight the factors and the resources of the company showing to what extent the company fulfils the critical success factors. The result then shows the competencies of the company.

CHAPTER 11

DOCUMENT/RECORD RETENTION

―――――○―――――

The retention of documents is essential, because it provides information to support decision-making by management, it also provides the following important facts:

- Record retention is part organisation policy which includes all types of documents and records created on behalf of the company as part of a business.

- It is essential because it provides information to support decision-making by management.

- In generally it's a legal requirement to retain records in the form of papers, files, electronic documents, correspondence (including letters, faxes and emails) and data used in business applications and databases.

- According to SOX; the retention of those records is necessary for oversight of the audit process, which enhances the reliability and credibility of financial statements for all public companies, and to facilitate enforcement of the securities.

Exhibit 11.1: Retention of Documents/Records:

Description	Number of Years
Detailed Costing Reports	5
Inventory Euros Change by Category Report – should include the Ranking of Inventory Changes Reports:	1
Labour Documentation – such as base rate scheduled, labour contracts, piece-rate schedules, minute standards, time studies used in setting rates, etc.	5
Raw Material Purchase Price Documentation – such as invoice copies of major material items, copies of price lists, summaries of purchases where average costs are used, etc.	5-6
Summary of Product Costs – should include material, direct labour, overhead, and total cost (electronic and or hard copy).	5-6

CHAPTER 12

CONCLUSION

This book is about putting the foundation of standard cost in place, to be used in product costing. By applying the correct standard costing, this book "Manufacturing Standard Costing Handbook" helps to understand the type of expenses that go into the right cost category, such as the following:

Direct Material - Materials that becomes an integral part of the finished product or which contributes to the fabrication and conversion of such materials (example in the automotive Steel, Aluminium, Plastics, Rubber, Spare parts), including materials used in packaging the product for sale.

Direct Labour – This is labour that, can be directly assigned to a particular item produced or which contributes directly to the fabrication of such product (example, welding, pressing, moulding, coating.

Factory Overhead - All other manufacturing cost that, cannot be directly identified to a given product such as indirect labour, factory supplies.

Variances are used to show the differences between budget and actual so that managers and cost accountants spend time on significant deviations from standards.

1. LACK OF MANUFACTURING STANDARD COSTING

I agree that implementing a standard costing system can be frustrating, labour-intensive especially if the cost structure of a production process changes, time-consuming, and expensive, especially for a small business. But can you imagine a business without a standard costing system, how would management decide on the price of a product?

This book, standard Manufacturing Standard Costing Handbook, was written base on the premise of using standard costs for product costing. Then, a lack of standard costs in a business would have a significant impact on the business, and the following are some of the examples if standard costing, is not followed:

i. BUDGET PLANNING AND CONTROL

The main reason why standard costing is implemented is because it helps businesses plan their annual budget. They'll use it to plan their output for the coming years, calculate the standard costs for materials, labour and overhead, that provides a guideline for future production expenditures.

ii. INVENTORY VALUATION

It is based, on the costs (direct labour, direct materials, production overhead, freight, import duties, handling charges) incurred by the business to acquire the inventory, convert it into its present condition that makes it ready for sale, and have it transported to the location of customers. However, in the absence of a standard costing, you may not be aware of the fundamental element of your product costs, i.e. you may include the administrative or selling costs into the cost of the inventories. Of course, this method of inventory is not allowed under any GAAP.

iii.   COST OF GOODS SOLD

It is the accumulated total of all costs used to create a product or service, and they fall into the general sub-categories of direct labour, materials, and overhead. COGS are calculated as beginning inventory + purchases - ending inventory. The assumption is that the result represents costs that no longer located in the warehouse; therefore, it must relate to goods sold. In reality, the calculation tends to assign too many expenses to goods sold, although, they were costs that relate more to the current period.

In the absence of standard costing, these extra costs assigned to the wrong period would have significant impact on the reported margin of the business or in worst case, your customers would buy the goods from your competitor, and this would cause severe issues to your business.

iv.   UNABLE TO COMPARE COSTS

It means that the comparison between the actual costs to the standard costs, and examining the variances between them would not be possible. Managers are not able to look for ways to improve cost control, cost management, and operational efficiency.

2. REAL-LIFE EXPERIENCE

I was once hired as a consultant to assist the incumbent Finance manager and implement the best-practise for the month-end close because it took them approximately 2-3 weeks to close their books.

The other thing that noticed was that they didn't have a formal standard costing system; instead, it was all done on an excel sheets and wasn't posted on any other system.

In my first month with the company, I had to close the books, including reporting. I began reconciling the balance sheet accounts, which were previously done once a year. I noticed that inventory reconciliations were also performed on an excel sheet, which of course tied up with the balances on their accounting software. That's because the reports came from the same system.

I decided that the company should perform a stock take to ascertain the actual value of their inventory. I obtained the product cost for all their products from their corporate HQ, which were then, single-handed inputted into their accounting system. After all the on-hand quantities of all the counted products, both onsite and off-site/consignment goods were entered into the system, the result was shocking. We realised that the spread-sheet Balance Sheet value was higher than the result of the count.

Due to the result of the count, it meant that we had to write down the inventory balance to reflect the actual value. Secondly, the other reason why we had to write down the value, is because, according to IFRS and US GAAP, if inventory is carried on the accounting records at a higher than its net realisable value (NRV), a write-down from the recorded cost to the lower NRV would have to be made. In essence, the Inventory account is credited, and a loss for the decline in NRV is debited to the cost of goods sold expense account.

3. RECOMMENDATION

- Standard costs should be revised every six months, or annually, or more frequently at the discretion of management, taking into account the cost/benefit associated with making more frequent revisions.

- Purchase price, material usage, and yield variances from standard costs for raw materials, packaging components, manufacturing/processing, and filling/assembly, etc., should be charged or credited to cost of sales (COGS) as incurred. These variances should usually be separately recognised and accounted for.

- The COGS standard should include a provision for losses which is to be reversed each month to offset actual losses during the month, except to retain. As a reserve, a sufficient provision for timing differences in the cycle counts.

- Differences between manufacturing labour and burden/overhead-related expenses absorbed by goods produced at standard versus actual production expenses during the fiscal year should be carried as deferred burden. If it is anticipated that the difference should not be absorbed during the remainder of the fiscal year, then the difference should be immediately charged or credited to cost of sales.

- Deferred burden should be adjusted to zero at year-end (charged or credited to cost of sales).

- Changes in standard costs resulting in material inventory write-ups should be credited to cost of sales over the future period corresponding to the turnover of the products whose cost has been increased.

- Inventory write-offs should be charged to cost of sales immediately and should be accompanied by an appropriate reversal of the loss provision accrued to anticipate such write-offs.

- Charges in standard costs resulting in inventory-write-downs should also be immediately charged to cost of sales.

- Variances between actual cost of sales and standard costs must be reported on a timely basis (i.e. monthly). Significant variances/trends, whether favourable or unfavourable, must be investigated and corrected as necessary to mitigate the potential for financial loss.

APPENDIX

APPENDIX A – GENERIC COST MODEL

JOB COSTING

	PROJECT
CUSTOMER: *Specification sheet* *Product number*	Job No.
City/ country/ delivery place Delivery terms: Delivery date:	Issued by/ on:
Total material only	Mat. Costs default	Mat. Costs Total Project
Direct Material	-	- -

Shipment		
Packaging / truck transport	0,00 %	0,00 €
Total		0,00 €

External work		
Manufacture (external)	0,00 %	
Total		0,00 €

Other		
Documentation/Software in customer's language		
Total		0,00 €

Material cost burden rate	0,00 %	

Total purchase		0,00 €

Production hours	Work hour rate	Hours	Hours	capital costs
		Standard	Project	
Assembly				0,00 €
Painting				0,00 €
Other				0,00 €
Total assembly				0,00 €
Electrical assembly				0,00 €
Electrical dismantling				0,00 €
Sonstiges				0,00 €
Total electrical assembly				0,00 €
Construction				0,00 €
Construction (planning)				0,00 €
Documentation				0,00 €
Total construction & documentation				0,00 €

Electrical project planning				0,00 €
Electrical planning operations				0,00 €
Testing				0,00 €
Other				0,00 €
Total electric		0,00	0,00	0,00 €
Total hours		*0,00*	*0,00*	0,00 €

Non-recurring costs	Work hour rate	Hours	
		Project	
Construction			0,00 €
Electrical			0,00 €
Testing incl.			0,00 €
Total			0,00 €

Total of production costs	0,00 €

Overhead costs

Sales		
Construction (development)		
Warranty		
Administration		
Overhead costs	0,00 %	0,00 €
Total costs	*(Cost price)*	*0,00 €*

APPENDIX B - BILL OF MATERIALS STANDARD COST FORM (BOM)

Appendix B:			**BILL OF MATERIALS - STANDARD COST FORM**						
			CH ERLIN CASINO TABLE, LG						
Date:			*21.04.2005*						
Requsted By:			*Niemanden Amreifen*						
Production / Ref:			*24560*						
Customer:			*F.Schmidta GmbH*						
Date Needed:			*01.12.2018*						
Address:									
Part No.	*Ne ed*	*QT Y*	*Material Needed*	*Co st Lev el*	*Direct*	*Dir ect*	*Manuf act.*	*Direct*	*Fixed*

102

			1	Mat. Cost	Lab. Cos t	O/He ads	Mach. Hr.	Expe nse
XYZ1	0		ASSEMBL Y OF COMPLE TE TABLE	- € 21 €	14 €	7 €		
XYZ2	1		A/ROULE TTE TABLE TOP COMPLE TE ASSEMBL Y	- €	- €	- €	- €	- €	- €
XYZ3	2	1 set	WHEEL SURROU ND BRASS, A/R TABLE L/H.	13 6 €	136 €	- €	- €	- €	- €
XYZ3	3		LEGS	- €	- €	- €	- €	- €	- €
XYZ3	4		FOOT RAIL	- €	- €	- €	- €	- €	- €

WXYZ4	5	1 set	DRINK HOLDER & ASHTRAY SOLID BRASS	154 €	154 €	- €	- €	- €	- €
WXYZ4	6		AIR RAILS	- €					
WXYZ4	7		CHIP RAILS	- €	- €	- €	- €	- €	- €
	8		PACKING	- €					
			This Level Costs	**310 €**	**290 €**	**14 €**	**7 €**	**- €**	**- €**

APPENDIX C - RECOMMENDATED PRODUCTION COST METHOD ESTIMATES

Determe Production Cost Estimates						
Example: Cost of Car Frame Sub-Assy (A day of assy-line production)						
Assemply Operations	Operation 1	Operation 2	Operation 3	Operation 4	Purchased Materials, Components cost	Total Cost
Type of Operation	Oper.1: Place to cut stock in length, & prepare for welding, + bend on bender.	Oper.2: Place to cut pieces in jigs forwelder, to remove welded frame from jigs.	Oper.3: To track & finish welding, prepared pieces for subassy.	Oper.4: Inspection, Cleanup, etc. for 8 hour shift.		
a. Total Time to Complete Operation(s) in Hours	3 Hours per Car Frame	1 Hours per Car Frame	1 Hours per Car Frame	0,5 Hours per Car Frame		
b. Labour Rate for the Operation	17,72 €	17,72 €	20,18 €	13,38 €		
c. Labour Cost = axb	53,16 €	17,72 €	20,18 €	6,69 €		
d. Basic Overhead Factor	1	1	1	1		
e. Equipment Factor	0,5	0,5	0,5	0,5		
f. Special Operation/Tolerance	0,25	0	0	0		
g. c x (1+d+e+f)= Labour / Labour /	146,19 €	44,30 €	50,45 €	16,73 €	100,00 €	357,67 €

APPENDIX D - SALES VARIANCE

	Volumes		Sales Price		Variances	Variance s	Sales Value	
	Month	Month	Actual	Forecast/ Budget	Eur 000	Eur 000	Actual	Budget
	Actual	Forecast/Budget	Price		Volumn Varianc	Price var	Sales 000's	
Product 1	59.951	45.580	160	167	2.400	(420)	9.592	7.612
Product 2	27.212	21.266	75	77	458	(54)	2.041	1.637
Product 3	9.136	4.891	180	182	773	(18)	1.644	890
Product 4	11.291	14.989	35	36	(133)	(11)	395	540
	107.590	86.726			3.497	(504)	13.673	10.679

Budgeted Results/Forecast			Actual Results	
Production /Volume			Production/Volume	
Product 1	45.580		Product 1	59.951
Product 2	21.266		Product 2	27.212
Product 3	4.891		Product 3	9.136
Product 4	14.989		Product 4	11.291
	86.726			107.590
Sales Value			Sales Value	
Product 1	7.612		Product 1	9.592
Product 2	1.637		Product 2	2.041
Product 3	890		Product 3	1.644
Product 4	540		Product 4	395
	10.679			13.673
Sales Price per Unit			Sales Price per Unit	
Product 1	167		Product 1	160
Product 2	77		Product 2	75
Product 3	182		Product 3	180
Product 4	36		Product 4	35

Selling Price Variance		Should have been (Euro)	But was	Selling Price Var.
Product	Volume	(Actual Sales Volume in Std Sales Price)	Euro	Euro
Product 1	59.951	10.012	9.592	-420
Product 2	27.212	2.095	2.041	-54
Product 3	9.136	1.663	1.644	-18
Product 4	11.291	406	395	-11

Sales Volume Variance		Budgeted/Forecasted	Actual	Var. in Volume	Sales Volume Var. in
Product		Volume	Volume	Volume	Euro
Product 1		45.580	59.951	14.371	2.400
Product 2		21.266	27.212	5.946	458
Product 3		4.891	9.136	4.245	773
Product 4		14.989	11.291	-3.698	-133

	Selling Price Variance	Sales Volume Variance	Actual Sales Varianc
Product	Euro	Euro	Euro
Product 1	-420	2.400	1.980
Product 2	-54	458	403
Product 3	-18	773	754
Product 4	-11	-133	-144
Actual Sales Variance			2.994

APPENDIX E - COST CLASSIFICATION BY FUNCTION

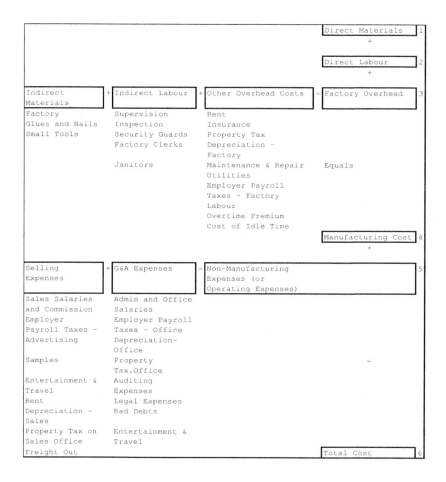

			Direct Materials	1
			+	
			Direct Labour	2
			+	
Indirect Materials	+ Indirect Labour	+ Other Overhead Costs	– Factory Overhead	3
Factory	Supervision	Rent		
Glues and Nails	Inspection	Insurance		
Small Tools	Security Guards	Property Tax		
	Factory Clerks	Depreciation – Factory		
	Janitors	Maintenance & Repair	Equals	
		Utilities		
		Employer Payroll Taxes - Factory Labour		
		Overtime Premium		
		Cost of Idle Time		
			Manufacturing Cost	4
			+	
Selling Expenses	+ G&A Expenses	– Non-Manufacturing Expenses (or Operating Expenses)		5
Sales Salaries and Commission	Admin and Office Salaries			
Employer Payroll Taxes - Advertising	Employer Payroll Taxes - Office			
	Depreciation-Office			
Samples	Property Tax.Office		=	
Entertainment & Travel	Auditing Expenses			
Rent	Legal Expenses			
Depreciation - Sales	Bad Debts			
Property Tax on Sales Office	Entertainment & Travel			
Freight Out			Total Cost	6

107

APPENDIX F - FIXED PRODUCTION OVERHEAD VARIANCES

PanSch GmbH Budget and Actual financial data for their last 4 Months

Description	Budget	Actual
Sales	1.000.075,20 €	970.072,94 €
Production & Sales Unit	100.000	110.000
COGS:		
Direct Raw Materials	140.110,96 €	135.907,63 €
Direct Labour	149.330,21 €	144.850,30 €
Production Hours	50.000	75.000
Number of Hours per Unit	0,50	0,68
Variable Production Overheads	95.591,81 €	92.724,06 €
Fixed Production Overheads	137.632,00 €	133.503,04 €
Fixed Production Overhead Absorption Rate (FOAR)	2,75 €	1,78 €

For simplicity, the above budget was prepared on the basis of 100.000 units produced and sold,
however, the actual production and sales for the four months period amounted to 110.000 units.
The company uses absorption costing.

Fixed Production Overhead Cost Variances:

Fixed Production Overhead Incurred	133.503,04 €	
Fixed Production Overhead Absorbed (€137.632/100.000 = €1,37)*110.000	150.700,00 €	
Fixed Production Overhead Expenditure Variance	17.196,96 €	(F)

The variance is favourable, because more overheads were absorbed.

Fixed Production Overhead Expenditure Variance:

Budgeted Fixed Production Overhead Expenditure	137.632,00 €	
Actual Fixed Production Overhead Expenditure	133.503,04 €	
Fixed Production Overhead Expenditure Variance	4.128,96 €	(F)

The variance is favourable, because actual expenditure was lower than budgeted.

Fixed Production Overhead Volume Variance:

Actual Production at Std. Rate (110.000 x €1,37 per unit)	150.700,00 €	
Budgeted Production at Std. Rate (100.000 x €1,37 per unit)	137.632,00 €	
Fixed Production Overhead Volume Variance	13.068,00 €	(F)

The variance is favourable, because output in volume (110.000 units) were greater than planned.

Fixed Production Overhead Volume Efficiency Variance:

110.000 units should have take (x 0.5 hrs)	55.000	
But did take	75.000	
Fixed Production Overhead Volume Variance in hours	20.000	(A)
x Standard Fixed Production Overhead Absorption Rate per Hour	2,75 €	
Fixed Production Overhead Volume Efficiency Variance:	55.000,00 €	(A)

Fixed Production Overhead Volume Capacity Variance:

Budgeted Hours Worked	50.000	
Actual Hours Worked	75.000	
Fixed Production Overhead Volume Variance in hours	25.000	(F)
x Standard Fixed Production Overhead Absorption Rate per Hour	2,75 €	
Fixed Production Overhead Volume Efficiency Variance:	68.750,00 €	(F)

The labour workforce worked 25.000 hours longer than budgete

APPENDIX G - MONTHLY VARIANCE ANALYSIS REPORT

Memorandum

Date:

To:

From:

Subject: Commentary Production Variance Analysis Report

   i.   Introduction

   ii.   Direct Material Price Variance $SQ (AP - SP)$:

- Favourable Reasons – Unforeseen Discounts Received

- Adverse Reasons – Price Increase, Careless Purchasing

   iii.   Direct Material Quantity Variance $SP (AQ - SQ)$:

- Favourable Reasons – Material used higher quality than standard.

- Adverse Reasons – Defective Material, Wastage, Theft.

   iv.   Direct-Labour Rate Variance $AH (AR - SR)$:

- Favourable Reasons – Used of less skilled (lower paid) workers.

- Adverse Reasons – Rate Increase.

v. Direct-Labour Efficiency Variance SR (AH – SH):

- Favourable Reasons – Better Quality Materials.

- Adverse Reasons – Lack of Training.

vi. Idle Time:

- Adverse Reasons – Machine breakdown, illness.

vii. Overhead Expenditure:

- Favourable Reasons – Cost Savings.

- Adverse Reasons – Excessive use of Services.

viii. Variable overhead variances:

- Unfavourable rate variance: Increase in costs, waste, theft, spillage, inaccurate standards.

- Favourable efficiency variance: The same as the labour efficiency variance.

ix. Manufacturing Cycle Efficiency:

= Processing Time X 100%

Processing + Time+ Inspection Time+ Waiting Time + Move Time

x. Manufacturing cycle time:

= Total Production Time per Batch

Units per Batch

xi. Recommendation:

APPENDIX H - DIRECT LABOUR

Standard Results			
Standard Units:	1.000		
Std Dir. Lab. Hours	Std Dir. Lab. Ho	Std Cost /Hour	Std Dir. Lab. Rate/Unit
Product 1	1,5	19,90 €	29,85 €
Product 2	2	6,00 €	12,00 €
Product 3	2	8,00 €	16,00 €
Product 4	2	10,00 €	20,00 €
Direct Lab. Rate			77,85 €
Actual Results			
Period:	5		
Actual Units Manufactured	1.600		
Actual Labour Costs	132.450,00 €		
	Direct	Indirect	
	Labour	Labour	Total
Salaried	71.987,86 €	25.548,00 €	97.535,86 €
Overtime - Basic	9.933,22 €	12.336,00 €	22.269,22 €
Overtime - Premium	0,00 €	699,00 €	699,00 €
Shift Allowance	0,00 €	2.385,00 €	2.385,00 €
Shift Premium	0,00 €	3.152,00 €	3.152,00 €
Sick Pay	0,00 €	4.289,00 €	4.289,00 €
Vacation & Holiday	12.562,94 €	9.080,00 €	21.642,94 €
Health Insurance	37.965,99 €	15.250,44 €	53.216,43 €
Idle Time	0,00 €	1.200,00 €	1.200,00 €
TOTAL PAYROLL	**132.450,00 €**	**73.939,44 €**	**206.389,44 €**

APPENDIX I - LIMITING FACTOR USING MARGINAL COSTING

A company manufactures two fashion jewellries Earrings and Necklacs. Unit variable costs are as follows:

	Earring	Necklace
	Euro	Euro
Sales Price per Unit	14	11
Direct Materials	1	3
Direct Labour (€3 per hour)	6	3
Variable Overhead	1	1
	8	7

During the year the available direct labour is limited to 8,000 hours. Sales demand in that month is expected to be as follows:

Earring	3,000 units
Necklace	5,000 units

Required

Determine the production budget that will maximise profit, assuming that fixed costs per month are €20,000,

and that there is no opening inventory of finished goods or work-in-progress.

Solution

Step 1   Confirm that the limiting factor is something other than sales demand

	Earring	Necklace	Total
Labour hours per unit	2 hrs	1 hr	
Sales Demand	3,000 units	5,000 units	
Labour hours needed (2*3,000 / 1*5,000)	6,000 hrs	5,000 hrs	11,000 hrs
Labour hours available			8,000 hrs
Labour Shortfall			3,000 hrs

Step 2   Identify the highest contribution that could be earned through it's limiting factor.

	Earring	Necklace
	Euro	Euro
Sales price	14	11
Variable cost	8	7
Unit contribution	6	4
Labour Hours per Unit	2 hrs	1 hr
Therefore, Contribution per Labour hour (= per unit of lim	3,00 €	4,00 €

Step 3   Determine the budgeted production and sales. Sufficient Necklaces will be made to meet the full sales demand, and the remaining labour hours available will then be used to make Earrings.

(a)		Hour	Hours	Priority for
Product	Demand	Required	Available	Manufacture
Necklaces	5,000	5,000	5,000	1st
Earrings	3,000	6,000	3,000 (bal)	2nd
		11,000	8,000	

(b)		Hour	Contribution	
Product	Units	Needed	per unit	Total
Necklaces	5,000	5,000	4,00 €	20,00 €
Earrings (balance)	1,500	3,000	6,00 €	9,00 €
				29,00 €
Less fixed costs				-20,00 €
Profit				9,00 €

Conclusion

a) Contribution by unit is not always the correct way to decide on priorities.

b) Labour hours are the scarce resources, therefore **contribution per labour hour** is the correct way to decide on priorities.

c) For example, the Necklace earns €4 contribution per labour, and the Earring earns €3 contribution per labour hour. Necklaces, therefore, make more profitable use of the scarce resource than the earrings.

APPENDIX J - JOURNAL ENTRIES FOR MANUFACTURING VARIANCE

Journal Entries for Manufacturing Variance

1. The general ledger entry to record the purchase of materials for the month is:

```
Raw Materials
    (12,000 units at €3.25 per unit) ..........  39,000
        Materials Price Variance
            (12,000 units at €0.10 per unit F) ...         1,200
        Accounts Payable
            (12,000 units at €3.15 per unit) .....        37,800
```

2. The general ledger entry to record the use of materials for the month is:

```
Work in Process
    (10,000 units at €3.25 per unit) ..........  32,500
Materials Quantity Variance
    (500 units at €3.25 per unit U) ...........   1,625
        Raw Materials
            (10,500 units at €3.25 per unit) .....        34,125
```

3. The general ledger entry to record the incurrence of direct labour cost for the month is:

```
Work in Process (2,000 hours at €12.00 per
    hour) ....................................  24,000
Labour Rate Variance
    (1,975 hours at €0.20 per hour U) .........     395
        Labour Efficiency Variance
            (25 hours at €12.00 per hour F) ......          300
        Payroll Payable
            (1,975 hours at €12.20 per hour) .....        24,095
```

113

APPENDIX K - MONTHLY OPERATIONAL KPI

Company   CH
GmbH

Month:	Jan	Feb	Mar	Apr	Mai	Jun	Jul	Aug	Sep	Oct	Nov	Dec
MRO Cost As % Sales												
MRO Cost (Maintenance, Repair, and Operating Supply)												
Sales												
MRO Cost %												
Target												
Utility Cost As % Sales												
Utility Cost												
Sales												
Utility Cost %												
Target												
Internal PPM												
Actual												

Target															
Supplier Delivery Performance															
Actual															
Target															
Inventory Turns															
COGS															
Inventory															
Inventory Turnover															
Target															
Scrap as a % of Material Used															
Actual															
Target															
Direct Labour Efficiency															
Actual															
Target															
Downtime															
Actual															
Target															

Mean Time Between Failure														
Actual														
Target														
Equipment Capacity														
Actual														
Target														
Changeover Time														
Actual														
Target														
Plant Overall equipment effectiveness (OEE)														
Actual														
Target														

APPENDIX L - MANAGEMENT COMMENTARY

COMPANY LOGO + NAME		
DATE: XXX 200X		
SUMMARY OF OPERATING PERFORMANCE		
Sales		
EBITDA		
Operating Cash Flow		
SALES		
	Variance	Comments
3rd- Party		
product 1		
Product 2		
Product 3		
COMMERCIAL & MARKET UPDATE		
Customer	Issues	
	Opportu nities	
Product	Issues	
	Opportu nities	

Market trends		
GROSS MARGIN		
Volume & mix	Variance	Comments Volume:
Production related		Example (Conversion cost, labour)
Variable selling expenses		
Total Variance		Gross profit variance
R&D	Variance	Comments
S&M		
Distribution		
G&A		
One off costs		
OTHER OVERHEADS		
	Variance	Comments

Other income & Expense		
Royalties		
FX		
IMPROVED OPERATING PERFORMANCE		
	Variance	Comments
Procurement		
Six Sigma		
CASHFLOW		
	Variance	Comments
Inventory		
Accounts Receivable		
Accounts Payable		
Intercompany		
Other working capital		
CAPEX		
	Variance	Comments
Cash out		
Under / (Over) Spend		
NOW EXPECTED (provide commentary on any material variances)		

	Variance	Comments
Sales		
Gross Profit		
EBITDA		
Operating cashflow		
NEXT MONTH NOW EXPECTED (provide commentary on any material variances)		
	Variance	Comments
Sales		
Gross Profit		
EBITDA		
HUMAN RESOURCES & ENVIRONMENT On time delivery close:		
Environment Health, and Safety (ESHA)		
OTHER		
Name: XXXXXX		
Title: XXXXX Date:XXX 200X		

APPENDIX M - HR KPI DATA

Company CH GmbH												
Month	Jan	Feb	Mär	Apr	Mai	Jun	Jul	Aug	Sep	Okt	Nov	Dez
Abwesenheit %												
Abwesenheitsstunden (stündlich)												
Abwesenheitsstunden (Gehalt)												
Arbeitszeiten (direkt)												
Gehaltsabrechnung Std. Admin (indirekt)												
Monatlich Ist-wert (direkt)%												
YTD Gleitender Durchschnitt												
Zielvorgabe												
Gesamtmitarbeiterzahl an Budget												
Monatlicher Umsatz €												
Indirekter Mitarbeiterzahl												
Direkte Mitarbeiterzahl												
Temp. Mitarbeiterzahl												
Tatsächlicher Personalbestand gesamt												
Budget (Gehalt H'Count)												
Budget (Hrly H'Count)												
Budget (Temp H'Count)												
Gesamtbudget für die Mitarbeiterzahl												
Ausfallzeit (Häufigkeitsrate)												
Verlorene Arbeitstage Fälle												
Arbeitsstunden												
Verlorene Arbeitstage Fälle pro 100 Vollzeitbeschäftigte												
YTD Durchschnitt												
Kontinuierliche Verbesserungsideen eingereicht												
Anzahl der eingereichten Ideen pro Monat												
YTD												
Ziel												

121

APPENDIX N - MANUFACTURING INDUSTRY KPIS

———o———

Improving Customer Experience & Responsiveness

1. Manufacturing Cycle Time:

It's the average length of time from the beginning of production to the FOB shipment of the product to the customer at an agreed date.

Manufacturing Cycle Time Formula = Process time + Movement time between processes + Inspection time + Queue time

Example: A car manufacturing Company recorded the length of time spent in the production of one of their products. The following information has been taken from the production department records:

Process time: 6 days

Movement time: 2 day

Inspection time: 3 days

Queue time: 2 days

The manufacturing cycle time is 13 days. It means that on average, the length of time from the start of production to finalising the shipment of the product is 13 days.

2. On-Time Delivery to Commit – This metric is the percentage of time that manufacturing delivers a completed product on the schedule that was committed to customers.

3. Time to Make Changeovers – Measures the speed or time it takes to switch a manufacturing line or plant from making one product over to making a different product.

Improving Quality

4. Yield – Indicates a percentage of products that are manufactured correctly and to specifications the first time through the manufacturing process without scrap or rework.

5. Customer Rejects/Return Material Authorizations/Returns – A measure of how many times customers reject products or request returns of products based on receipt of a bad or out of specification product.

6. Supplier's Quality Incoming – A measure of the percentage of good quality materials coming into the manufacturing process from a given supplier.

Improving Efficiency

7. Capacity utilisation is the percentage of capacity that is actually used from anticipated capacity. It is calculated using actual output and capacity:

capacity utilisation = (actual level of output / Maximum possible Output) × 100

A car manufacturer has an assembly capacity of 10.000 units a week. They're currently running two shifts and producing 1.660 units a day.

capacity utilisation = (8.300 / 10.000) × 100 = 83%.

8. Throughput – Measures how much product is being produced on a machine, line, unit, or plant over a specified period of time.

9. Overall Equipment Effectiveness (OEE) – This multi-dimensional metric is a multiplier of Availability x Performance x Quality, and it can be used to indicate the overall effectiveness of a piece of production equipment, or an entire production line.

10. Schedule or Production Attainment – A measure of what percentage of time a target level of production is attained within a specified schedule of time.

Reducing Inventory

11. WIP Inventory/Turns – A commonly used ratio calculation to measure the efficient use of inventory materials. It is calculated by dividing the cost of goods sold by the average inventory used to produce those goods.

Formula: WIP Inventory/Turns

Total Cost of Goods Sold / ((Inventory Value of WIP at Start of Measurement Period + Inventory Value of WIP at End of Measurement Period) / 2).

Example:

Cost of sales per day: 619 + 795 = 1.414

Average WIP 20X9: 1296.0 + 1309 = 2.605 ÷ 2 = 1.303

) WIP Inventory/Turns: 1.414 / 1.303 = 1.1

Ensuring Compliance

12. Reportable Health and Safety Incidents – A measure of the number of health and safety incidents that were either actual incidents or near misses that were recorded as occurring over a period of time.

13. Reportable Environmental Incidents – A measure of the number of health and safety incidents that were recorded as occurring over a period of time.

14. Number of Non-Compliance Events / Year – A measure of the number of times a plant or facility operated outside the guidelines of normal regulatory compliance rules over a one-year period. These non-compliances need to be fully documented as to the specific non-compliance time, reasons, and resolutions.

Reducing Maintenance

15. Percentage Planned vs. Emergency Maintenance Work Orders – This ratio metric is an indicator of how often scheduled maintenance takes place, versus more disruptive/un-planned maintenance.

16. Downtime in Proportion to Operating Time – This ratio of downtime to operating time is a direct indicator of asset availability for production.

Increasing Flexibility & Innovation

17. Rate of New Product Introduction – Indicates how rapidly new products can be introduced to the marketplace and typically includes a combination of design, development and manufacturing ramp up times.

18. Engineering Change Order Cycle Time – A measure of how rapidly design changes or modifications to existing products can be implemented all the way through documentation processes and volume production.

Reducing Costs & Increasing Profitability

19. Total Manufacturing Cost per Unit Excluding Materials – This is a measure of all potentially controllable manufacturing costs that go into the production of a given manufactured unit, item or volume.

20. Manufacturing Cost as a Percentage of Revenue – A ratio of total manufacturing costs to the overall revenues produced by a manufacturing plant or business unit.

21. Net Operating Profit – Measures the financial profitability for all investors/shareholders/debt holders, either before or after taxes, for a manufacturing plant or business unit.

22. Productivity in Revenue per Employee – This is a measure of how much revenue is generated by a plant, business unit or company, divided by the number of employees.

23. Average Unit Contribution Margin – This metric is calculated as a ratio of the profit margin that is generated by a manufacturing

plant or business unit, divided into a given unit or volume of production.

24. Return on Assets/Return on Net Assets - A measure of financial performance calculated by dividing the net income from a manufacturing plant or business unit by the value of fixed assets and working capital deployed.

25. Energy Cost per Unit – A measure of the cost of energy (electricity, steam, oil, gas, etc.) required to produce a specific unit or volume of production.

26. Cash-to-Cash Cycle Time – This metric is the duration between the purchase of a manufacturing plant or business unit's inventory, and the collection of payments/accounts receivable for the sale of products that utilize that inventory – typically measured in days.

27. EBITDA – This metric acronym stands for Earnings Before Interest, Taxes, Depreciation, and Amortization. It is a calculation of business unit or company's earnings, prior to having any interest payments, tax, depreciation, and amortization subtracted for any final accounting of income and expenses. EBITDA is typically used as top-level indication of the current operational profitability of a business.

28. Customer Fill Rate/On-Time delivery/Perfect Order Percentage - This metric is the percentage of times that customers receive the entirety of their ordered manufactured goods, to the correct specifications, and delivered at the expected time.

Printed in Great Britain
by Amazon